How to Comm
Relatio

Learn The Secrets to Improve your Communication skills and Finally living a successful relationship

By Mark Hooper ©2020

Copyright Page

Introduction

Communication is ship on which relationship sails.
Not many people are aware about their communication flaws until they get to discover that lack of communication effectiveness was their undoing. Don't allow this to happen.
Things can quickly go sour when effective communication is missing in a relationship. It is the tool that binds friendship, builds marriages and helps you understand the other person better. How effectively you're able to communicate make you win in the time of trouble and crisis.
You mustn't allow your relationship to suffer. Get all you need to know about effective communication to make it solidly founded on a solid ground. It is not in the talking but by action. You must stand up against any breakdown in your relationship via communication inefficiency.

How to communicate in a relationship is an insightful book designed to cover every aspect of everyday needs as regards communication. By reading this book, you'll learn the basics of communication and how it applies to build a good relationship. Its content are well-structured to assist the reader understand effective communication as it affects the growth of a relationship. The first part of the book takes the reader through the meaning and types of this invaluable tool while the second section teaches the reader how to improve communication. The book gets more specific in the third and final section exploring the various exercises and games you can use to enhance your communication efficiency in a relationship.

You can take your readings from the top or jump over to any chapter in the book as you so desire as they can be independent of the previous one. Digest and take action!

Disclaimer

The information provided herein in this book is not made to replace the place of any form of professional advice, or legal or other professional services, as may be required. The content and information in the book has been given for informative and educational purposes only.

The information contained in the book has been collected from sources believed to be reliable, and also correct to the best of the knowledge of the author. However, the Author cannot pledge its accuracy and cannot be alleged liable for any errors or/and omissions. Furthermore, alterations are occasionally made to the book when needed. Where suitable or/and necessary, you should consult a professional before adopting any of the suggested techniques exercises, or information in the book.

By using the contents and information contained in this document, you agree to hold the Author responsible from and against any penalties, costs and expenses, including any legal fees that may arise from the use of any of the information contained in this book. This disclaimer refers to any liability, or harm arising from the use, directly or indirectly, of any advice or knowledge received.

You agree to accept all risks associated with using the information presented within this book.

You consent to contact a specialist (including but not limited to your psychiatrist, lawyer, or financial advisor or any other expert if needed) before using any of the recommended strategies, exercises or details in this book by continuing to read this book, where applicable and/or required.

Table of Contents

PART I - WHAT IS COMMUNICATION? HOW TO CREATE IT IN THE BEST POSSIBLE WAY

The subject of communication in a relationship may not sound new but with changes in the world we live today, new things continually unfold as regards how the subject is treated. What does communication mean in our current age? This section takes you through the details; clearing your doubts and helping you understand the basics.

CHAPTER 1: What communication means in relationships?

Communication is as old as man, and an important part of our lives and interactions with people. Even the creator, according to Biblical accounts, engaged in physical interactions and communicates frequently with the first man on earth to run the affairs of the world at the time.

Therefore, life can't be lived to its fullest without communication. Even animals communicate to co-exist peacefully within the eco-system. Nature interacts with plants, as much as man interacts with plants and nature itself.

Interestingly, man communicates with nature as much as he interacts with his fellow man. For instance, humans interact with the air, which supplies oxygen for life. In the same vein, humans breathe out carbon dioxide, which is useful to plant.

This analogy simply tells us about the multifaceted nature of communication and also emphasizes how interactions or relationships between creations in the universe ensure world order. Therefore, it is hoped you will be inclined to agree that communication is essential for our everyday life. What oxygen is to human life is what communication is, to our social lives. It is a world of interaction.

Before getting deep into the real issues for this book, it is important to examine what communication truly is in our days.

What is communication?
Communication, like many other terms, has been defined using different perspectives. One definition that captures its meaning is the transmission of information between two people or groups of people. It can also be defined as the use of mutually understood signs or symbols to send a message.
Communication is used in everyday life in different fields of life endeavors. The market women, the office attendance, students in the college, the poor and the rich, the educated and the illiterates, the professional and the unskilled labor and the list goes on…it's a world where everybody is involved.

Right from when you awake in the morning to the close of the day, your transactions are done by communication. You begin by saying 'good morning' to your loved ones in the home to saying, 'this is the best way to get the job done' in the office and to 'how much does it cost' in the grocery store and finally say 'good night' to cap things up for the day. The summary is that a good part of life is spent every day in communication. Life will appear meaningless without it, it is like the gas used to power or machines.
Where your relationship is today can be attributed to how well you've mastered the art of communicating effectively.

Communication has components:

There is no communication without certain channels or systems in place. They are elements that link two or more entities together.

For instance, there must be a sender, a channel or medium through which the message is to be sent, and there is a receiver, to whom the message is sent. You can pick from here that there are three basic components but sometimes a channel of communication can come in between. This is where various media types such as the use of paper, phones and mass communication media come in.

While there are three basic channels of communication, one of these components remains the most important. It is one component that tells you that communication has taken place. So, if you ever try getting your message to someone, never think you have communicated and completed the cycle if the message was delivered. Surprised? It shouldn't stop there. Feedback is essential.

That is only when you'll be able to tell that the message was truly received. You have truly communicated when your message is followed by a feedback from your receiver.

In a nutshell, communication has the following components:

Relationships are built on communication

Now, that you know what it is that makes up communication and why it is an essential part of your life, how is it like in your relationship? Is it standing on a solid ground?

Take it or leave it, communication is the bedrock of every relationship; it depends on how well you've used it to impact the relationship. It is the connection you need for your relationship. From the very first date to the time you both smiled to the altar, communication was that pillar. How you were able to woo her in the first place was the power of communication at play. Can you vividly remember the first reaction you got from her? That is your feedback right there. She reacted because she got a message; that was the feedback you needed to prove that the communication was effective.

Without a doubt, it is the oxygen that fuels every human relationship. To be more specific, communication in relationships involve the mastery of, and intentional application of verbal and nonverbal skills to fulfill the emotional or physical needs of one's spouse, a child, the parent or other relation, friend or other members of one's social circle. It is misleading to only think that this definition applies to spousal relationships alone. Every human connection is a relationship; either it is sexual, social, spiritual, professional or casual.

You just need to be there when it comes to communication in relationships.

Relationships often come with expectations and some responsibilities for each party or individual. It is for you to play that part the right way. Thus, a proper mastery of communication skills is important for meaningful human interactions. Communicative skills, which are often divided into verbal and nonverbal skills, can be learned like every other skill. That is why you shouldn't just sit there without learning. You must learn the correct application of communicative tools in the right context or situation.

Communication comes with understanding

You communicate frequently but many things can still go wrong when understanding is lacking.

In relationships, communication can be described as understanding each other. The point of emphasis here is that communication in a relationship is basically about understanding her.

Consider this analogy: A professor of communication enters a class of first-year students, at a college for students with hearing impairment. The professor begins to apply verbal skills to teach students, but he realizes that his teaching didn't resonate with the students.

He also saw that he couldn't connect with the students. As soon as he noticed this, he switched to using sign language, and the first feedback was that the students began to beam with smiles on their face. Based on this analogy, the ability to connect with one's listener is the prime factor in any relationship where communication exists.

You must go beyond just speaking many words which don't build up, get her to understand what you're passing across to her.

Communication requires that the communicating parties share some areas of commonality; your relationship is that bond. Remember the scenario painted above; the use of sign language helped to foster understanding and deepens the relationship between the professor and his students. Can you imagine how it feels listening to a preacher, who spends 5 hours preaching in a service largely constituted by teenagers, whose attention span isn't more than 2 hours or less, in some cases? The only time a communication process is complete and effective is when there is mutual understanding or a sense of commonality.

Ways of Establishing Understanding in Communication

Who are you dealing with?

It is not the same way you talk to your child you are going to converse with your colleague in the office, NO. They are two worlds apart. Likewise, the language you use for your spouse will be quite different from how you discuss with your friends.

Having full knowledge of the other person is important to your success in communicating effectively. If communication is going to be effective, it is the audience type that drives it. Is your audience a boyfriend, spouse or family member in this case? Get it at your minds back to have a picture of the person you're communicating with. It determines your choice of words, the tone and voice and the emotions that you'll be attaching to it. The affection comes to light more in a love relation in your conversation but more civil when in a professional environment.

Your audience demography such as age, gender, and other physical characteristics is one key factor to consider in effective communication. Communicate in their level, don't ignore this.

As you hope to become a better communicator, one skill you must develop or master is the ability to appeal to your receiver's emotions. You can succeed at this when you send a message or tell a story that your receiver can connect with.

Tell a story

Storytelling is one of the ways one can improve understanding in communication, tell the story.

One of the most ancient and most time-honored forms of communication is storytelling. People have told each other stories for ages to help them understand the world, anticipate the future, and certainly to entertain as well. The art of storytelling draws on your understanding of yourself, your message, and how you communicate it to an audience. Go back memory lane and recount the events to her, the first time you met and things you did then. Your anticipation, reaction, and adaptation to the process determine how successfully you can communicate. Everyone has a story to tell, and if you tell your story well, you are sure going to get listening ears.

Be open-minded

Don't have a hidden agenda at the back of your mind when in communication with her, it won't help your flow. Not too long, she will get to know you're only making up stories. You don't have to agree all the time, don't pretend to. When you do, endeavor to reach a middle ground between which you can air your views and pass across your message without disregarding hers.

A successful communicator will build a deep relationship with the listener and get the desired action.

Top Communication Skills

To help the other person to understand you, learn how to communicate effectively.

Growing your communication ability requires developing some skills. They are called communication skills because they foster effective communication. You need them to get your message across to her more effectively.

1. Cohesion and clarity

You know effective communication by its clarity. It has cohesion and passes across the intended message clearly without misleading the receiver. Before you even begin to talk, know exactly what you want to talk about and go straight to the point. This will yield a better result. When you communicate your message across in a cohesive manner, it helps you avoid conflicts of thoughts and your listener tends to follow you better. Clarity of purpose in communication aligns with straight-talking. This builds mutual trust. To be clear with your communication, say only what you mean and mean every bit of what you say.

2. Listening skills

Listening is a top skill to help your communication. A good listener not only understands the content of a message but also feels and connects with the speaker in the course of the conversation. How do you feel when you find that your audience is carefully listening and following your conversation? You feel excited and happy, don't you?

You also get encouraged to keep going with your thought in confidence when you listen more than talk. Listening is very important to communication and this is the reason we'll get deeper with more details as we progress.

3. Stress management

Many relationships suffer shipwreck not because partners had serious issues but they fail to manage the stress effectively. When stress management suffers and stress seems to have taken over completely, it affects opinion clarity and behaviors and actions during communication. Your decision suffers and you obviously won't be enjoying the relationship especially when it is a romantic one. The ability to manage stress helps your relationship. When you are under stress a lot of things happen to your communication. It can ultimately lead to the end of a relationship.

4. Emotion control and intelligence

Communication and feelings work together. Your feelings get more to influence a decision than what you think about a person. Controlling emotions puts you on top of things to better understand the other person, the messages you send and others you are talking with. Being able to manage your emotional intelligence helps you overcome stress, challenges, and have empathy with others. This skill is learned over time and not what you obtain. Emotional intelligence comes with self-management, social awareness, relationship management, and self-awareness to help your effective communication.

5. Tone

Every communication is different based on who you're talking to. The tone in your voice carries a lot of meanings. Use it to let her understand better. Your tone during communication can determine the mood of the conversation. Watch it. If you're aggressive, expect that your partner will respond in the same way to you. The voice can include a whole lot of things including your emotion level, and the level of communication you bring to play.

Don't let your listener think something different. Your words can mean something more with the tone and voice that comes along with it, let it be a positive one if you're looking to build a good relationship.

Getting the right voice and tone to speak with is important to your effective communication. Depending on the environment you're in, the voice and tone can be any of friendly, formal to informal. You need an affectionate voice when dealing with your lover; a formal one in the office and a friendly and informal tone for friends and family including neighbors around.

6. Confidence

Got this? Many have failed in life because of a lack of confidence in themselves. Demonstrating a high level of confidence is important to your effective communication. How do you bring confidence to play in your communication? One effective way is your composure and eye contact when conversing with a person. Being firm and talking straight, but friendly shows you know what you are talking about; be confident about what you say.

7. Empathy

We are different have different views of life and how things should be done. With empathy, you can understand the other person and where he or she is looking at things from. Empathy makes you respect other people's views. With empathy, you don't see your colleague or friend to be wrong but rather respect whatever point they have raised. Empathy helps you to respond appropriately this way.

8. Asking Questions

Questions help to build communication and understanding. Ask questions to help the flow and enhance the outcome of your conversation. Open-ended questions are good for conversations, make sure to ask to help the flow and ensure you're not alone in the conversation. Questions encourage people to bring out other points and with more explicit responses; you can get further clarifications, thus, boosting understanding.

So what skills are yet in the top rank for detailed consideration?

Communication is about everything in a relationship. You should nurture it so it grows. You can only build a good relationship when you have a good grip of this important skill. But you must be a good listener to master this very important art. What does it take?

CHAPTER 2: Effective listening: communication starts here

In the previous chapter, so much is said about communication. A point worth emphasizing on though is that communication has to be effective. This simply means that the message yields results for which it is intended.

But the fact is, you must first listen to communicate effectively.

How well you're able to listen to your partner when she talks determines how effective your communication will be- effective listening breeds effective communication.

Listen with rapt attention to know how to respond adequately.

It is possible for you to be a good communicator, but you only become an excellent one, when you become a better listener. The ability to listen effectively is the responsibility of not only the sender but also, the receiver of the message.

No matter the effort the speaker or sender of the message puts into sending a good message or information, the receiver of the message has the responsibility to listen well. It is when this is done, that communication really takes place.

Don't be in a hurry to talk, be the good listener first.

Just like it was earlier said, understanding is important in building effective communication in relationships. But the truth is, there is no understanding without listening or some form of paying attention to the message being communicated or sent. Imagine a husband comes home from work, tired and hungry. He then requests that his wife (who is very much engrossed in her favorite television program) gives him a cup of coffee with milk. But because she is distracted and not listening well, she brings him a cup of coffee with a bottle of honey. Clearly, the television program is a distraction or a barrier to the wife's ability to listen.

7 Tips to Help you Become an Active Listener

1. Have an open Mind

For you to listen effective during a conversation, you must have an open mind. Quickly jumping into conclusion won't pay you any good but can lead to strive. Don't look for the right or wrong during a discussion if you want to make your listening count.

2. Prioritize listening

To prioritize listening, you must leave your agenda behind. Keep aside what you have to say and concentrate on listening to the other person first. Avoid all the distractions around even if you're in the living room where you have gadgets around.

3. Don't Interrupt

Make sure to allow your partner conclude what they have to say. If you have this shortfall with interruption during a discussion, adopt some means to prompt to not interrupt the other person. A practical way you can adopt to do this is to put your chin in your hand. This will prevent you from speaking until your partner has concluded.

4. Keep focus

Exactly how are you going to listen when you don't keep focus? That will be difficult. You need to keep focus all the time. The major point that is being discussed should be one you must mind to keep in mind. It is absolutely in order to ask question if that will help to focus more on the point raised.

5. Have a good knowledge of your communication style

Every discussion may come with a different communication style. Being aware of the different styles you use during your communication can aid your ability to listen well to your spouse or partner. Likewise it is okay that some individuals have distinct way of speaking. You should know your partner's mode of communication and style. This will help to improve your listening power.

6. Pay attention to signs

You have distinct signs that both of you are familiar with. Pay good attention to them when your partner is talking. The signs can be any of tone voice, shrugging of shoulders, nodding, crossing of the legs or arms and different facial expressions such as smiling, frowning, surprise and rolling of the eyes and a whole lot of others. Know that more than half of the message tend to be pass across will come by signs and non-verbal expressions.

7. Use Feedback Techniques

Feedback techniques lets your partner know that you heared what he said. You can use words such as 'I heared what you just said.' The feedback technique can be the non-verbal signs described above. Common feedback techniques include nodding of the head as a sign.

Poor listening skills are a major obstacle to effective communication. Without listening there can be no understanding of the message. There are so many barriers to our ability to communicate well with family and friends.

Barriers to Listening

The roadblocks to good communication in relationships are many. Whether you are trying to use technology, words, symbols or signs, no matter the method of communication, there are always barriers that make it difficult for communication to be effective. Some of these barriers are things we use on daily basis for life's conveniences in the home.

Technology as a barrier to Listening

The same technology that makes it easy for you to interact with our loved ones, can become a barrier to effective listening. For instance, a video game, television soap, a sound system or even a bad network can make it difficult for you to listen well or be listened to. A schoolboy whose mom is helping with his assignment cannot listen well to the instructions he is given if he is distracted by a video game. A waiter may mix up the orders if she is distracted by her favorite television soap, while she is taking orders over the phone. Even more, poor signal or network from telecommunication service providers may affect one's ability to send or receive information over the phone.

• Choice of words as a barrier to Listening

It is not the time to pour out all the college vocabularies you've learnt in your life. Conversations in relationships should be simple and make for easy connection between the two of you.

When you use complex words or terms that are difficult to understand, you make it difficult for your partner to understand your message. Words that are the same but have different meanings, can often be misinterpreted. To avoid this, then you must ensure that your partner gets the intended meaning through careful words choice that avoids the possibility of multiple interpretations.

Another point to note is that you must ensure that the language of your message is well suited for the context, in which you want to use them. You should never use expressions suited for informal conversations or interactions, for discussions that relate to business, or finance.

Also, age or demography appropriate language is important. The words that are suited for conversations with children are different from what you will when talking to older people. You will never be able to get people to listen to you if your language is not right.

Behavioral / Physiological challenges as a barrier to Listening.

Some changes in your emotions or how you feel can affect how well you listen. A sad student may not listen well in a classroom -check your emotions and temperament. The same way a hungry congregation member may not listen well to the minister's sermon.

Physiological barriers like ill health, poor eyesight, or hearing difficulties may affect one's ability to listen. As a matter of fact, a common cold can impact someone's ability to compose or understand a message properly.

Environment as a barrier to Listening:

Some environmental factors may affect one's listening ability. Some of these environmental factors are room lighting, weather or atmospheric temperature that can impede listening. For instance, in a corporate setting, one can do a few things to allow for better interaction between customers and the company's representatives, by ensuring that the room or reception is cool and well ventilated. This, in return, will encourage alertness.

Techniques For Reducing or Avoiding Listening Barriers.

While there will always be obstacles to our ability to communicate well and listen well, we can reduce or in some cases, avoid completely, these barriers. This book will suggest ways that will help you become a better listener here.

There is no hard and fast rule to these listening strategies, but your ability to apply them within the right context, and to the right audience, can make all the difference. Some of the measures you must consider are explained in the headings below:

Minimize Distractions

Whether you are sending a message across to an individual or group, or you are the listener, you must learn to reduce internal or external distractions. I have categorized these distractions under internal and external distractions.

Internal Distraction -An internal distraction is when you as a speaker is receiving a call while making a presentation, and this can make it difficult for your listeners to concentrate.

External Distraction- On the other hand, an external distraction which may be caused by a listener, or a group of listeners will affect the concentration of other listeners. An example is a baby crying or throwing tantrums, while a presentation is going on, or an individual is talking.

 This external distraction (a crying baby) just like the internal distraction (dragging of feet by the speaker or ringing cell phone) will affect you and whatever role you are taking in communication- as a sender or receiver of information.

Practice Reflecting and Story Telling

When you intermittently allow for reflection, occasional pause, share personal experiences, you can get better engagements from your audience. Stories appeal to people's emotions, and when you tell your stories well, you are sure going to get people to listen to you more. There is a need for you to take caution: keep your stories as brief as possible.

Here is the final advice on how to achieve better listening

Use Visual Aids or Attention Grabbers

You will make it easy for people to listen to you, or achieve better social or sexual relationships when you help the person listening to you visualize what you are trying to tell them. When it comes to dealing with children, one method that will help, as a parent, for instance, to get their attention is images or visuals.

This is so for adults too. We can always differentiate between an item that says so much about losing weight, but we can resonate better if we find one that shows us what we will look like in 6 weeks. If one is trying to lose some belly fat, and will personally find it easier to buy produce that catches my attention and appeals to my senses- sight or any other sense that is applicable.

Indeed the starting point of every communications should be listening. How well you listen tells how well your communication will make sense to the hearer. Get this working for you at this stage to give your communication a good foundation.

There are so many strategies or techniques, but what is important is to apply them. You can make out of your interactions better listeners or become one yourself as long as you practice. Indeed, practice makes perfect.

CHAPTER 3: Speaking to make yourself understood, proactive dialogue

There is more to just speaking out words. Engaging in a proactive dialogue puts you in charge. You understand the other person and knows where he or she coming from. There is a mutual connection between the two of you. This is the time to talk about you and the family, the kids and other issues in the home. It is not the time to start talking about the office.

The message must be clear before there can be a listener. So, as much as you will want to agree that listening is necessary for communication to take place, speaking with clarity can make understanding words, sounds or symbols or any medium of communication easier. The words you choose when you communicate must be clear and precise. If not, your words can easily be misinterpreted.

Language and Clarity

Language is broader in scope

Communication in a relationship is about language and not speech. Language doesn't have to be expression of words only. There is body language, the language of love in a romantic relationship and many other languages whether verbal or non-verbal in a relationship.

Language is not the same as speech. Language is not limited in definition, as speech is. Language involves the use of words, signs, symbols, written texts or oral messages to send information or communicate. Devise your own language in your relationship that your partner will connect better with in your relationship. She should understand you without you saying a word when the understanding is there.

For example, sign language is a kind of language, just like verbally expressed words. A sign language interpreter will have no problem communicating with a congregation of people who are all literate in the language. But the deaf who is not educated or literate in the use of signs and symbols will never get the message, but if he or she can write, or read and understand texts written in other languages, such as English, he or she will have no difficulty communicating or being understood. Therefore, language is broader in scope; it is not limited in the definition.

Language is phenomenal

Language is beyond words or symbols alone. It is a phenomenon that even the birds of the air, the animals in the wild understand. The bird knows when to fly because the weather communicates with it; the fish knows when to swim deep or shallow, the animal knows when to hunt or stay away from hunting; so it is for the flowers, they know the best time to open, so it is for every other creation. Language is present everywhere, and its message can be understood in varying contexts. You both connect in language, otherwise, there won't be any relationship or if there was, growth in the relationship will be in question when language is missing.

Language and Dialogue

A dialogue is possible between two people when they there is mutual understanding in language. It must be the language you both understand. As you have professional jargons in a field of endeavor so are words that reflect your type of relationship. Discover them and use them to boost your relationship. Let's go beyond the literal language here. This is about relationship and how you connect with each other.

Just as it is possible to have conversations or meaningful dialogues when we speak in native languages or tongues, you can engage symbols, signs and shades of passing on your message across more effectively. You see it is possible not to understand a language, or speak it, but one can be fascinated by the manner of dialogue, especially if you can tell that the two conversationalists are communicating well!

So, the dialogue is present in every language, at any place and at any time. Speech is only a form of language which involves the use of spoken words or verbal expressions. Speech is limited, language is not. Speech is a form of human communication that involves the use of spoken words or articulate sounds. It is also the expression of thoughts or ideas through articulate sounds. A speech like other forms of human communication involves the use of language.

How to Speak Clearly

To speak clearly, you must bear three basic things in mind.

• Speak slowly and articulate your words carefully.

• Do not speak too fast, as this may pose a difficulty to your audience's ability to understand your message.

Every dialogue has a style

Our words, through oral communication basically serve to inform, or persuade. You may have read or heard of different definitions or categories of speech, but, of all, the basic categories are persuasive and informative speeches. Your relationship should be spiced with a variety of words and communication styles.

As much as you can, use more informative dialogue, interactive communication than persuasive methods in your conversation.

While persuasive speeches attempt to influence people's thoughts or opinions about an issue,

Informative speeches seek to sensitize or educate people. Relationship is more about sharing ideas and thoughts, don't send a wrong signal to your partner on a communication style that doesn't fit into your relationship type. Make your partner feel at home, allow empathy take root in your conversation. Be willing to take her own views of life and embrace ideas that will build your relation further.

Every speech serves a particular purpose, depending on the context. The kind of communication style you choose for a conversation should fall in place appropriately to match up with the conversation style. Determines the kind of dialogue or engagement one receives from the audience or listener.

Speech and clarity

When a message is clear, irrespective of the purpose of it, whether to inform or persuade, the listener can engage or follow the dialogue. Therefore, you can't have a meaningful engagement with your partner without dialogue. In order words, clarity is what produces dialogue.

As a communicator, you must be able to fulfill some requirements for proper communication to take place. For instance, you should speak in a clear and easily understandable manner.

Also, the purpose of the speech must be clear. There should be a connection between what you as the speaker expects, and what the receiver expects. This understanding is what produces meaningful dialogue.

Opinions may differ

It is not enough for you to speak clearly, those listening to you must agree with you or disagree as the case may be. It is when this happens, that you can have better engagements or productive dialogue.

Please you should also understand that sometimes, a purposeful dialogue can also produce arguments or disagreements. It is proper for you and your partner to disagree. Things can be resolved using the same power of communication.

A nurse, who is educating women about sleeping positions during pregnancy, for instance, may have meaningful disagreements with some of the patients' views. Or in some other cases, it may be the patient, in this case, the listener, who may disagree with the nurse's positions.

When this kind of opinions arises in a relationship effective communication through dialogue will help the situation.

Disagreements, dialogues, and clarifications

If your partner ever disagrees with you when you speak, it is never a time to argue any further. It may be an opportunity to pause, take a deep breath, and make appropriate clarifications.

Many men go into their defensive cocoon as soon as their listeners disagree with them. An excellent speaker must not only speak with clarity, must not become defensive, but engage or re-engage his partner in order to achieve a purposeful dialogue at the end of any communication exercise.

Tips for meaningful dialogues or conversations

As this chapter, draws to a conclusive end, you can learn a thing or two from the tips shared below:

•Identify your subject area: don't just speak broadly. Know what you intend to address in your lives. There should be something very pressing in your relationship that needs attention. Ensure that you are knowledgeable about the subjects that interest or may interest your partner. If you are not knowledgeable about teaching Chemistry never take a Chemistry class or attempt to become an instructor for one. That is usually the saying and it applies more also in relationships.

•Understand your partner: Know the kind of subjects that appeal to your partner or what you need to discuss. Find out long before, the type of discussion or if an informative talk will resonate with them.

•Choose a place: The setting for the chosen conversation or dialogue matters. Never talk about business or have a conversation about making business deals at a brothel. It is simply out of context. It is also ridiculous to consider asking a lady out for a drink during a church service. The wrong conversation, wrong place, and conflict are certainly set to ensue. Generally, conversation spots should be peaceful locations.

•Listen before you speak: A good speaker must first be a good listener. Listen to your environment, the weather, things that are said and unsaid. If you listen or pay attention to your partner's body language, and the environment or atmospheric condition, you are likely to have a more productive dialogue.

Hope these tips help. So far, we have looked at communication, its definition, and its history. We went ahead to talk about understanding as the key aspects of communication. We have also explained how important listening is in communication and relationships. Some of the distractions to listening have been explained too. But what exactly are the different types that are out there.

Your communication should rest on a proactive dialogue where the other person understands everything you say. Being proactive helps you to place strong priority on the discussion and thus enhancing understanding for the communication to be effective. Are there other ways to effective communication?

CHAPTER 4: Ways of communication: verbal, paraverbal, kinesthetic, assertive, persuasion, negotiation, manage conflicts, body language

Communication, as earlier said, has an age-long history. Therefore, the different ways of communicating in relationships and interactions have an age-long history.

While the different ways of communication have been modified over time, across societies, the systems or channels of communication have not changed. These basic channels of communication are, always and every time, sender, message, and receiver. However, technology-mediated communications are among the newly developed systems of communication.

There are different perspectives on the ways of communication. However, some have been identified and are to be discussed here.

Ways of Communication

We have identified some ways of communicating, among others. Although, other writers may propose a few of these, let it be said that communication is an evolving thing that grows. Things get added as the years' passes. After you have read about the ways of communication suggested here, you may be able to come up with other or use a combination of a few, in your relationships and interactions.

Broadly speaking, communication can be divided into two categories of verbal and non-verbal communications. Other subdivisions come out of these major two.

Verbal Communication

This is one of the oldest forms of communication, which cuts across borders, race or cultures. Verbal communication involves a combination of words and sounds. This form of communication also involves the use of words to share information with other people. It can, therefore, include both spoken and written communication.

However, many people use the term to describe only spoken communication. The verbal element of communication is all about the words that you choose, and how they are heard and interpreted.

Among the many other kinds of verbal communication that may not be listed here, are intra-personal communication, interpersonal communication, small group, and large group communication.

Intra-personal Communication

The word 'intra', a Greek language expression, means inward. Therefore, intrapersonal Communication is a form of communication that is extremely private and restricted to us. This type of communication can be likened to a monolog. Did you read Shakespeare's Hamlet?

If you did, do you remember the scene where Hamlet was applying this principle? Sometimes, we need to first have intra-personal communication or conversation with ourselves, to examine how we treat our spouses or loved ones. In some other cases, we should examine how people treat us when we have this honest conversation with ourselves.

Interpersonal Communication. This form of communication takes place between two individuals and is thus a one-on-one conversation. This is one form of communication that solidifies our relationships with our loved ones. Everybody in life needs interpersonal relationship.

Small-Group Communication. This applies to the formal conversation.

Public Communication. This is also applicable to formal settings.

What differentiates small group or large group is the number of those who make the group. Such communication settings are generally categorized as formal settings.

Paraverbal Communication

Paraverbal Communication has to do with the sound, pitch, and tone of our conversation when we speak. It is also a set of messages, instructions or information that we transmit or send out, using the sound, tone, and pacing of our voices. Some of the components of paraverbal communication are pitch, sound, and voices.

Pitch

Pitch is how high or low your voice goes.

Speed or cadence

This has to do with how fast or slow, you talk.

Tone

This is a combination of factors that set or convey meaning.

Scenario: A relationship can be further sustained or destroyed through wrong or misinterpreted paraverbal signals. So, the next time you are speaking, take care not to speak in the wrong tone, pitch or even try not to speak too fast.

The essence of communicating with your partner is to be understood, not misunderstood or misinterpreted.

Even when you don't notice, our speeches are packed with a combination of paraverbal communication features. Every speech has a pitch, which can be termed the volume or frequency of our internal sound system (speech organs such as tongue). The speed with which we talk may affect the pitch. Even more, we can tell if a speech will be fast, from the tone of the speaker's voice.

Kinesthetic Communication

Kinesthetic communication, as the name suggests, is the act of communicating with the body parts. Most times, our body language helps us to describe some messages, that may not be best expressed with our words. In romantic relationships, many times, if not all, a good hug, a pat on the cheek, makes all the difference or sends messages that our words may not communicate effectively.

Even parents use this medium of communicating to show love, encourage or instill discipline in their children.

It is amazing how much we can achieve, if romantic partners or lovers deploy this communication style, effectively.

Purpose of Communicating: Assert, Persuade, Negotiate, etc.

We have discussed in detail, the different ways of communicating. Now, let us look at the various reasons people want to speak, or communicate. They are numerous but we have. Identified three other medium of communicating, which are for clarity, and assertion,

Assertive Communication. We express some messages or information when we apply one or more ways of communicating, to show our authorities, and power. An assertive speech will be characterized by one or more paraverbal communication features- such as a high tone, speed of communicating and or pitch.

Persuasive Communication

When we speak with our loved one, to help them see the need to stop a behavior, or course of action, we can achieve this set goal, by persuading them. The tone, speed or pitch of a persuasive speech, is different from that of speeches aimed at serving other purposes.

Negotiating Communication

Once upon a time, a speaker said: "every person is in the business of negotiating every day, from the baby crying to get the parent's attention", to a student wanting to understand a concept from the teacher, where the tone of voice is different from others in all cases. It is the voice and the choice of words here that makes the difference in this situation.

Communication Styles

The way humans share ideas with each other through a language is a style of communication. When it comes to style of communication everyone is different. Several factors such as history, age, regional location and education affect our specific style of communication.

It can be tough to understand others at times, they apply different styles. At one stage, you may think that you are sharing the same information, but in fact, you're far apart in your thought. These can lead to conflicts which can interfere with a good relationship.

It goes to say that knowing the different styles helps to respect others during conversations, remember empathy.

Your gender can be another factor. Men including women interact with each other in unique ways. Do you realize that for the behavior of women, it is softer? May we say that they were made to live the gentle soft spoken life? It could be.

Explore your personality then, and know how you interact with other people. Know how your personality influences your friendship, as well. Make a check of yourself if your personality is such that your wife disagrees with you or causes you more tension in the relationship.

You can follow a style, or practice a particular style or even a combination of different styles in your relationship.

That said, a look at some communication styles stated below can help your communication.

Affiliative Style Vs Competitive

You appear to want to work more collaboratively with people in the affiliate style of the communication. Through sharing your experiences with one another, you get problems fixed rather than moving ahead with them. This is a good style to adopt in a relationship since it considers the input of everyone involved. When you share thoughts with your friend to seek his view before making a final decision, you are the associate or affiliative communicator. You might also see this person going ahead to explain the same thing to friends and family before taking decision on some matters.

A competitive communication on the other end appears to claim power and dominance. You don't want this for your relationship. Those with that communication style are much more blunt and demanding. Men may tend to be in this category most times. Rather than getting any views or contributions from others they prefer to make their decisions.

You will figure out where you fit in between these two and make the needed change where necessary. A good way to know about this is to ask yourself some relevant questions. It will guide you in knowing where you are going to fall.

• Do you prefer to make decisions without your partner getting involved?

• When you're given any information, do you speak up immediately or listen to hear other side of the story?

• How exactly do you feel in situation where others contest power with you?

Sincerely respond to these questions to know where you stand in style.

Condensers Vs Amplifiers

Amplifiers will say a lot as they give information. They simply want to say more in a limited time. Many sentences are employed as well as the use of descriptive words. It's distinct from simplified communication where one or two sentences satisfy the communicator. A simplified communicator is most relaxed with only half of what's needed to say. Generally, as with most amplifiers, 70 percent of women fall in this group while the men are condensers. Of course there are situations where the man can be the amplifier in marriage, and the woman is the condenser.

For a condenser husband, too many words from an amplifier wife may be disturbing. Sometimes, an amplifier might feel frustrated that a person is not speaking much or too quiet about his partner.

Whatever party you belong to, you should both follow a way of striking a balance in your relationship. As a condenser communicator, see yourself as complementing the other person and not as a competitor.

Hot Vs Cold Style

The conversation type in conflict resolution in a relationship has various aspects to it. A lot of people belong to the group with hot communication styles. The hot communicator kind of person will often come out straight and get it dealt with immediately. He needs it to be done right now.

Conversely, the cold communicator is never in a panic. He is the type who wants to go away and consider problems for a moment and weigh different options before finding a suitable answer. He does not like being coerced into any action.

What are you? Probably you fall in-between the two.

You shouldn't treat any style as superior to the other.

Direct Vs Indirect

Communication can either come as direct or indirect communication.

Have you seen those people who talk really directly? They don't go playing around the bush; these groups say it and hit it right from the start. They prefer to be very frank about what they think, or want to do. For instance, "I'm going to see the head teacher now,". That statement is easy to understand.

In direct communication, it is very simple to understand what the communicator is doing. This type of communication, when in a relationship, is very direct and intuitive, but sometimes can be a bit harsh.

Indirect situation it is a little slightly more subtle and less formal. An indirect communication does away with all sorts of abuse. Perhaps, the communicator would say, "I think that seeing the head teacher tomorrow will be a good idea for us." Although an ambiguous comment may be subtle, it may sometimes be more tolerable than coming out blunt.

In addition, everybody uses the direct and the indirect forms of communication at one time or the other. Nevertheless, a lot of people go with one of those models than the other. In a romantic relationship, particularly among married couples, it's common to find women leaning towards the indirect form of communication than the direct form.

Use any of the two as the occasion demands.

The chances of misunderstanding are addressed when you use the most direct communication. With those two forms of communication, stress and conflict are not uncommon in the relationship if you don't know how best to deal with your partner.

Handling Differences

For each individual in relationships the communication styles will be different. It does not mean though that these relationships should be governed by disputes and disagreements, NO. Such communication gaps make it interesting, and should be viewed as such. You might find your partner is drawn to you because you are the dominant form. The place of understanding and flexibility is what makes those relationships stick together.

When you know how your friend interacts, you are more likely to pay attention and knowing his style, relationships flourish because both sides understand the other.

If you're open about how you see the two of you talking, you'll build a better friendship this way.

Once you find out what your style of communication is, it's time to look at how you can use it to build a good relationship with your partner with aim to help reduce your stress level and improve your relationship. If making a change in an area is vital, go ahead and gradually bring the changes into your communication style. When you enjoy your friendship, you should not succumb to the rigidity of communication; there should be space for adjustments to prevent stress.

There is so much to learn from the various ways of communication. They help you to apply different communication styles, all of which helps to make your communication effective. Apply each communication principle as it fits well for your conversation. But another vital point of note is getting the connection right and respecting other people's views is key to effective communication. This is empathy.

Managing Conflicts and Body Language

The primary focus of communicating well is to be understood. Sometimes, misinterpretation can occur if the messages or words are not well organized. When this happens, we may not be able to get the outcome or expected reaction.

When we're trying to navigate difficult situations – especially those that involve a conflict of some kind – we're very careful about the words we choose but what about our body language?

Sometimes we focus so much on what we're saying that we forget to think about how we're conveying it. And importantly, what our body language and facial expressions are communicating to the other person.

Practical Ways to reduce conflict

We can't overemphasize the need to have some practical strategies that will help us communicate in an enjoyable and fulfilling communication exercise. Here are a few ways to practically reduce the chances of misunderstandings in communication or body language misinterpretation.

• Your words, your body language: To avoid conflicts in our interactions or relationships, endeavor to consciously bridge the gap between your words, and your body language. In order words, ensure that there is synergy in your expressions.

•See another perspective: Good communication always begins from the ability to see things from the other person's point of view. Then listening to understand the other person's words and body language, is the beginning of a healthy relationship.

CHAPTER 5: Empathy and connection: the keys of communication

Communication is much easier with some invaluable features there to help us. You should not view yourself as having all the knowledge in the world, others may right too in their own way. Understanding empathy allows you to see others views more clearly to connect with them.

Think of other people's perspectives

You're probably familiar with the saying, "Walk a mile in their shoes before you judge others." Examine your own mindset, and keep an open mind. Too much focus on your own beliefs and assumptions doesn't leave much room for empathy!

When you "see" why other people believe what they believe, you can work better with them. This doesn't mean that you have to agree with it, but this isn't the time for a debate either. Alternatively, make sure to show respect, and continue to listen.

The trick to coping effectively during crisis is to connect with people in a real, human way.

Knowing the feelings of other individuals is a key skill within the workforce. It can help us to resolve conflicts, create more efficient teams and deepen our partnerships with co-workers, consumers, and clients. In relationship, empathy is key and needed to make the difference.

What is Empathy?

Empathy in its simplest form is the ability to recognize feelings in others and to understand the viewpoints of others on a situation. Empathy at its most encourages you to use that experience to boost the attitude of someone else and to help them during challenging situations.

Empathy is often associated with sympathy, but it is not the same thing. Sympathy is someone's feeling and a hope they might be happier. Empathy means understanding and respecting the views of your partner.

You may feel sympathy for someone you see on the street who is in tears, without understanding their circumstance. Empathy doesn't mean to agree...

Empathy is the ability to put oneself in someone else's shoes: connecting with and recognizing someone else's emotions, feelings and experiences. This does not mean that you truly agree with the person. Demonstrating empathy means you're trying to understand, and trying to help someone else feel heard.

Empathy isn't complex, but it isn't simple too. Why not common?

Types of Empathy

Emotional Empathy

Emotional understanding is the ability to share another person's feelings, and thus to comprehend another person to a deeper level. It is sometimes referred to as "affective empathy," as it influences you. It is not just about understanding how somebody feels, but about building genuine relationships for them.

That kind of empathy can be daunting for some of us. Persons with strong empathic tendencies may get engulfed in problems or suffering from other persons, often harming their own emotional well-being. This is especially true if they feel incapable of resolving the situation.

Through taking breaks, testing your limits and improving your ability to cope in such a demanding role, you will stop this kind of emotional breakdown.

Anyone who leads a team will benefit from at least some human intelligence development. It helps to build trust in management and team members, and establish openness and honesty. But when it is paired with behavior, empathy is most important.

Cognitive Empathy

Cognitive empathy is the capacity to understand what another person might think or feel. It need not require the observer's emotional involvement.

Managers can consider cognitive empathy helpful in knowing how they feel about their team members, and thus what leadership style they would get the most. Likewise, sales managers can use this to gauge a customer's attitude, helping them choose the most appropriate tone for a discussion.

Cognitive empathy is an ability that is most logical, analytical and emotionally balanced. Which means some people are using it for negative purposes? For instance, those with a Machiavellian personality trait may use cognitive empathy to exploit emotionally vulnerable individuals.

Compassionate Empathy

The more powerful type of empathy is conscientious empathy. This means not only being worried about another person, and expressing their emotional pain, but also taking concrete steps to reduce that.

Suppose, for example, that one of the team members is upset and angry because he or she poorly delivered a major presentation. It is important to accept their pain and to reinforce their response by showing signs of those emotions. But the best thing is to give them some patience to provide practical support or advice to get through the crisis and plan for the next time.

How to Build Empathy

You might initially fail to show empathy—you might be worried about emotionally sacrificing yourself, or feel unable to do so. But that does not mean you're doomed to failure in your relationship since you need this to grow.

To make effective use of empathy, you will put aside your own point of view and see things from the perspective of the other person. You can then recognize behavior that seems to be overly emotional, defensive, or irrational at first glance as merely a response based on a person's previous knowledge and experiences.

Frequently use the following methods so that they continue to become second nature.

Listen and Listen

Pay attention to what somebody is trying to tell you. Use your mouth, eyes and "good instincts" to understand the entire message they are sending.

Begin watching out for the keywords and phrases they use, particularly if they consistently use them. So talk about how well they speak and what they do.

Go on with this one stage by listening empathetically. Do not ask direct questions, disagree with what is said or challenge evidence at this point. And be versatile-prepare to change direction for the discussion as the thoughts and feelings of the other person do change.

If in question, encourage the individual to explain their situation a little more, and ask if they think they can solve the problem. Presumably, the easiest and most straightforward way to understand the other person is to ask the right questions.

Take Action

There's no "right" way to show off empathy. It'll depend on the situation at the time, the person, and their dominant emotion. Keep in mind that empathy is not about what you want, but about what the other person wants and needs, so any action you take or propose will help them.

For example, you might have a member of the team who is unable to concentrate on their job due to an issue at home. It may seem like the kind thing to do to reassure them that they can work from home until the situation is resolved, but in reality, work will give them a welcome break from worrying about something traumatic. Then ask them what solution they'd like.

So know empathy isn't just about disasters! Seeing the world from a variety of perspectives is a great talent-and in any case, it is one that you can use all the time. And random acts of kindness make everybody's day happier.

You often smile and take the trouble to remember the names of people, for example, that's empathy in practice. Giving people full attention in groups, learning about their lives and desires, and giving constructive feedback are also both empathic behaviors.

Also, exercise those skills. If you're involved in what others say, sound and experience, you're going to develop a reputation for being thoughtful, trustworthy and open-minded.

Let people know you listen before moving on.

Discipline yourself to take the' extra' step of restating, paraphrasing, or somehow verifying you've heard and understood them before going on to the next subject, or before describing yourself. It speeds down the conversation, but if it is too noisy it can help to lower the tension and will hopefully save time in the long run.

Have you got empathy in your communication skills? If not, it is essential skill to add to your skillset in the communication subject. People will respect you for this because you have regards for their views. Empathy helps to improve your communication skills. There are yet other ways to improve your communication skills. Let's get to meet them.

PART II - IMPROVE COMMUNICATION SKILLS IN YOUR LIFE

The ability to communicate effectively is never static, it grows. You too can improve your communication skills in diverse ways. This section highlights the various ways and techniques that work to enhance your communication efficiency. Read on…

CHAPTER 6 : Communication skills at the workplace: 5 ways to practice oral communication

It is important to note that active communication is what keeps the world going. Cities interact with cities, nations to nations and people to people.

You cannot achieve much in isolation and if it takes active communication to become a better person in life, then you must understand all it takes to be a good communicator.

When it comes to the work environment, communication is very important.

It is like the oxygen that you breathe that keeps your life going. You can't thrive in your workplace either as the boss or employee without good communication skills. You work with people and they must be able to understand you and every instruction that you may want to pass along.

"But I talk too..."

Yes, you do talk, but clarity and understanding of what you talk about are key. A lot of bosses come to board meetings and just talk for a period of 2 hours without checking if their message is clearly understood by their employees. A lot of people go to work and come back more confused about what exactly their bosses expect from them because something went wrong; communication.

Are you that kind of boss? It's time to learn and unlearn.

How do you go about it?

Listening

You can only be a good communicator by being an active listener; this is one of the key statements in this book.

Thought communication is about talking... Not at all!

How do you do that?

• Avoid concentration on your phone or any other gadget like pads and laptops during a work-related conversation

• Look straight into the eyes of the person that is talking to you

• When responding, make sure you rephrase their points

Language and Nonverbal Communication

Body language speaks a lot of volume at the workplace. A sensitive speaker will identify a lost listener in a meeting. Make sure to follow every work-related conversation with your eyes, body, and mind. If you're tapping your fit on the floor, it may mean you can't wait for the speaker to end his speech and this may cause you problems at your workplace if you are the employee.

You're the boss, listening to your employees is very important too. Nobody wants to work all night over a report and is just about to share it with a boss and the boss is not attentive or unresponsive. Your communication power can help build or negatively affect output in the company.

The negative attitude from a boss can lead to:

• Lackadaisical attitude to work

• Loss of confidence

• Low self-esteem

• The feeling of not being appreciated

• Possible resentment

If you work in a client-based establishment where you have to deal with customers every day, you must learn the listening skill. That way you're able to genuinely listen to the client's complaints about your product and services and you're able to relate them to the appropriate department for enhanced customer satisfaction.

The customer is satisfied, an increase in company productivity and a possible rise in your salary!

Who doesn't want that?

All you need is just key communication skills that will enhance your performance at work.

Communication resolves conflict

Listening helps you resolve conflict at your workplace. Most of the quarrels and fights at workplaces are a result of a misunderstanding.

If you are in a heated argument with a colleague, rather than raise your voice, listen to what he is saying and perhaps, when you understand where he is coming from, you may be able to communicate a solution to the cause of the crisis.

By just having a simple conversation with your colleague where you both listen to each other, you will discover that there was no issue in the first place.

You can understand the personality of people by simply listening to them.

Establish Workplace Friendship

There is no harm in establishing friendships at your workplace, your workplace is supposed to be fun too.

Ask how your colleague is faring

Check up on your sick employee

Communicate disappointment in a less harsh tone

Compliment your colleague's new look

Compliment hard work and give rewards

Don't bear a grudge for too long

Doing all of these is you trying to be friends with people at your workplace. When you talk to people, you give them the confidence to approach you, and when you are approachable, people can easily give you professional advice that will help you grow in your career.

The friendlier you are, the easier communication gets! Arm yourself with workplace virtues.

Be Audible

When you're addressing your employees or colleagues, be sure to be loud enough for all to hear from you. Adjusting your voice to be heard in various settings is an effective communication skill.

When you're addressing a team of 10 people, your voice should not be in the same tone as when you are having a conversation with just one person.

You will agree that professors who do this in high school tend to have half the class dozing or sleeping by the end of the class.

You don't want to be a boring person at your workplace, so practice voice modulation to understand how loud or how low your voice should get when addressing people at your workplace.

You should also be careful not to be unnecessarily loud such that instead of people listening to your ideas, they are irritated by the nuisance of you are making of your voice.

Be audible so that your ideas and suggestions can be effectively passed across with clear understanding.

Precision

Always pass your suggestions and ideas in a clear and concise form. Don't go about ranting and repeating the same thing in a conversation with a colleague or meeting to the point that your point is not understood.

Hit your point with precision, such that whenever you're talking, people will be interested in what you want to say as you're not regarded as a time-waster.

Respect

Respect people enough to allow them to air their opinions and suggestions. In teamwork, you should not make everything about you and you alone.

Allow other people to talk. Ask them clear questions and don't jump to another topic without patiently listening and responding to their thoughts before jumping to another topic.

Remember communication is not centered on you alone but between you and other people in your workspace.

Empathy

Learn to put yourself in the shoes of people rather than condemn them. Identify when someone is feeling frustrated or angry at difficult tasks in the office and help them with ideas that could bail them out.

You can say things that will relieve their tension, giving them room to rationalize the best way out of that situation.

When there is a disagreement, being able to understand the other person's point of view towards work progress is empathy.

Prompt Responsiveness

You must respond promptly to the task given to you at the office. Your slackness can be termed as lack of interest, laziness or lackadaisical attitude to work.

When assigned a task, read thoroughly to know how soon you are expected to deliver, work within the time frame of delivery. If it's a task that would take you a long time to deliver, respond with an mail to indicate you've acknowledged it and you are already working on it.

What are the 5 Ways to Practice Oral Communication?

Practice makes perfect

As old as this saying is, its truth is everlasting. You should practice your speech particularly when you're to give a presentation at work. Don't assume you already know it, stand in front of your mirror and read out your points.

You can record it on your phone and listen, again and again, to be sure you're not missing any point.

If you intend to establish a fresh conversation with a new colleague at work the next day and you're not sure of being confident enough, get a friend and have them act as your new colleague, and act the scene.

You don't want to look stupid in the presence of a new employee. Having read through all these skills, it is important for you to know how to practice oral communication to improve relations at your workplace.

Having read through all these skills, it is important for you to know how to practice oral communication to improve relations at your workplace.

1. Frame your Thoughts in exact words

One of the errors of communication is not being able to properly express your thoughts with the right words.

You understand what you're saying, but the people you're talking to are not able to grasp what exactly you are talking about.

Your language must be simple enough for people to understand after all the essence of communication is being able to convey your thoughts and express yourself to people.

So be sure to practice this often and with time, you will find that you're no longer difficult to understand.

2. Get Past The Fears of Making Grammatical Errors

Do you refrain from talking at work because you are scared you could make mistakes and be embarrassed?

Mistakes are part of learning, so it is not an abnormality in communication. The more reason why you should talk more so you can identify the areas where you make these common mistakes and make corrections.

You may experience difficulty at the initial stage, but with proper tutelage and guidance, the errors of yesterday will be corrected and not be repeated today.

3. Stop Being Hesitant

A lot of people due to self-esteem issues tend to count themselves unworthy of taking the microphone. Don't listen to the voice of your weaknesses! If you know you've got something reasonable and progressive to talk about at work, don't hold back, Say it!

Be less concerned about people's perception of you or the way you look. At the end of the day, your looks don't speak, your voice does.

Break past that fear and speak up!

4. Develop a Healthy Reading Habit

There are lots of benefits that can be derived from reading.

When you read, you are exposed to new vocabularies that will aid your oral communication skills. When you look up those new words in the dictionary, a new world has been birthed into your brain, particularly when you use it in subsequent conversations.

When you read, read out loud sometimes so you can hear yourself pronounce some difficult words. Compare your pronunciations with that of an audio dictionary, so you can be sure you're not going to pronounce the word wrongly during a presentation at work or a conversation with an unfamiliar colleague.

5. Learning from movie Scenes

Don't rule out learning from movies, yeah! There are lots of English speaking movies that you can watch and learn up new words and expressions.

It's an unconventional form of reading, it doesn't have to be all on prints, grab a drink and a jar filled with popcorn at your leisure and enjoy great movies and at the same time learn how best to communicate in a different context.

In a movie, you will see different scenes play out from formal to informal scenes and this will show you the appropriate trend of communication for each.

Communication at the workplace is key to improving your relationship with people as it defines your personality and performance in the long run. You must be able to communicate your opinions and suggestions properly without ignoring other people's opinions.

You should ensure eye contact and mind your body language when talking, and when you're being spoken to so you are not misunderstood.

Do you want to have a beautiful work relationship at work? Follow all of these steps and in no time, your workplace will be one of the best places you want to be.

CHAPTER 7: Effective communication in marriage: how it works

Effective communication in marriage is very important for any marriage that will survive the turbulence of family life. You must be dedicated to getting this right if you must have a successful marriage.

In most cases, how far a couple last is determined by their level of communication which brings a high level of understanding of each other.

Most marriages crash to divorce because at some point, the couple in question couldn't communicate or stopped communication in the marriage.

Communication in marriage is like oxygen or fuel that keeps the engine of love running.

Foundation laying

If you are reading this as a single, about to get married, you must understand that the foundation of effective communication In marriage must be laid during the courtship period if the marriage must last.

A lot of people go into marriage with the hope of getting things right there. This is a big mistake!

When you consummate your relationship and get married, it is just a one-day event of initiation into a legal cohabitation. So nothing practically changed between the two of you. So the marriage starts as a continuation of your courtship.

So no magical wand was used to do any abracadabra of any sort to change what wasn't there.

Initiate the kind of communication flow you want to continue in your marriage. Study your partner and know what works for them and doesn't. you can know a lot about your partner during courtship if you dedicate the time to it, it not that difficult.

Know what your partner's love language is,

Favorite hangout spots,

Favorite sport

Favorite meal

Favorite color

The kind of gifts that will be appreciated from a lover's perspective (you may love the gift of a customized pen, but feel more loved with the gift of a vase of roses)

Avoiding the Negatives

Negatives in communication in marriage are the things that can spark up unhealthy reactions in your marriage. A lot of people do things that constantly offend their partners without knowing.

Never sleep on a grudge

When you are angry with your spouse over something that was done wrong, do not sleep on it. The minute you bear that grudge to bed, it will affect your communication. You may even decide not to have sex out of anger, and that is putting your romantic life at risk.

Politely relate what you were not comfortable with, apologize if you were wrong, and move on. That way you will most like get clarity on the issue, and sometimes it may be a simple misunderstanding. But the minute you sleep over it, the offense has tendencies to multiply, you will start seeing unnecessary underlying factors responsible for the grudge and if not well managed, you will start building resentments that are not healthy for a marriage.

Avoid Dirty Fights

When you do have quarrels, make sure not to use dirty languages or use your spouse's failure to spite them during quarrels.

Words are like eggs. Once let out, it gets shattered and cannot be amended. Even after you say sorry for saying awful things to your spouse, the words and your expression when you said it can never be erased from the memory.

So be careful with your words and mind the things you say. Your words can either make or break your marriage. If your marriage is worth keeping, you may begin to check the things you say amid a fight. Don't miscommunicate!

Quit the Blame Game

Please know that taking the blame is never fun, and when you are always watching out to blame your partner, you are communication 'pseudo perfection'. You are simply saying you are always right and your partner is always wrong.

Be objective in conflict resolution. It doesn't matter who is right or wrong, what is most important is being able to resolve your issues without making your spouse feel bad about the whole scenario.

Avoid Making Excuses

A lot of marriages crash because one person never takes responsibility for his/her fault. Once it is crystal clear that you are wrong, accept it and simply apologize.

If you forgot the keys to the house in your office, simply accept the fact that you forgot it. Don't tell your wife it was her fault because she asked you not to come back home late.

She did no wrong by asking you to come home early, you didn't argue that it wasn't convenient but now that you have forgotten your keys, it has suddenly become her fault?

In the same vein, don't take the blame for what you didn't just for peace to reign. It will do you a great disservice in the long run. Anytime you accept responsibility for what you did not do, you are communicating weakness and gullibility. And this may expose you to be taken advantage of in your marriage.

You don't have to share any blame, be objective, apologize, make amends and everybody will be fine.

Apart from the ones listed above, do a soul search and check what you regularly do that communicates a wrong message to your spouse and causes quarrel.

Hey! You should avoid all of these negatives and make your marriage work, communicating the right things.

Effective Methods For Effective Communications

Keep the Flame

People generally complain about how care and love in their marriage dwindle just after their wedding. A lot of times, people tend to be more caring during courtship but once they get married, they become too familiar with their spouse and forget the very things that kept the fire of their love burning.

Don't kill the fire, against all pressures and overwhelming responsibilities of marriage and family life, take out time to show love to your spouse.

You can keep the flame by doing Love projects from time to time. Write one amazing thing about your spouse daily or weekly and show it to him or her at the end of the month. This will light a love spark and communicate your emotions beyond your imaginations.

Whenever you are in the circle of friends, never speak negative things about your partner, tell them of how amazing and terrific he is. Words go round you know!

The positive things you say about your partner has a way of getting back to him or her. It shows you place your marriage on a high pedestal of love and understanding. The feeling is invaluable when your spouse hears of the valuable things you say about him or her in town.

Reaffirm your love for each other in the face of conflict. Don't go about spilling regrets about settling for your spouse in the middle of a quarrel. That may put a dent to your marriage and cause your spouse to begin to doubt the sincerity of your love for him or her.

" I'm so pissed at the moment with you, you should change this attitude!

You are an amazing and adorable person and I am grateful for the gift of you, but I'm pissed"

With this kind of bittersweet admonition, your spouse will feel the need to change in respect for the love that you both share.

Develop Healthy Love Habits

There are love habits that you can also develop to spice up your marriage.

• Develop a habit of saying "I love you" at the end of every call with your spouse
• Choose a day in the week for romantic dates
• Kiss your spouse first thing in the morning
• Send love messages to your spouse while at work
• Be deliberate about making every anniversary special (This includes wedding anniversaries, birthdays and valentine's day)
• Send gifts to your Spouse's workplace (It communicates love)
• Take a long walk with your spouse at weekends

These and many more you can habits you can form to foster beautiful communication between your spouse and you.

Do not allow Gadgets put you Asunder

Technology has its positive side and negative side. At least through it, you can call your loved one through mobile phones, do video calls, exchange messages within a short time without having to walk down or travel down.

People live in different cities and country and they can still maintain a healthy flow of communication, all thanks to technological inventions.

But

This same phone can also lead to challenges in marriage. A lot of people ruin their marriages because they have not set their priorities right. If your marriage means a lot to you, you should be wise about how much time you are spending on your phone when your spouse is around.

When you go out to dinner, it's best you leave your phone in the car or switched off in your pocket or bag to avoid distractions.

Why ask your spouse to date when you have an online meeting with your business partners around the same time?

Why choose to check up celebrity gist blogs while at a date when you should be looking into your spouses' eyes over a glass of wine?

Don't play video games alone while your partner is left staring at the ceiling of the house all by herself or himself.

Make sure to carry your partner along and whenever you say you're going out to have some fun time. Don't make it about your phone, your iPad, texting and exchanging emails.

It can be very boring, and in the end, you would have communicated the wrong message of "you're not as important as this" to them.

Learn to use your gadgets wisely.

Clear Expectations

Don't always assume your partner's response to a situation. Always seek their opinion on every matter. It gives a sense of belonging and that their opinions are as equally respected.

"Honey we will be going to Dubai for our next vacation, I hear it's a beautiful place I got us tickets already."

"Honey, what do you think about us going to Dubai for our next vacation? I heard it's a beautiful place"

In the first statement, you are assuming for your spouse, leaving him/ her with no option than to either follow what you want or refuse and this can cause a conflict. I am sure you don't want that.

The second statement is not assuming, it is you asking for your spouse's opinion and that communicates respect and involvement.

Even if you can guess what your spouse's response or choice will be on a particular matter. It is still nice that you seek their opinion and not assume.

Be an Active Listener

In as much as you love to be understood, it is also important that you understand your spouse too.

When having a conversation, listen attentively with an open mind to understand your spouse's point of view. Don't listen with a premeditated answer, and just watch him or her blab.

Listen to understand, process their line of thought and give your perspective, not you discarding their explanation and just lording your opinion without actually listening.

Your spouse will know if you have listened to them by your subsequent responses.

"So what do you want to do now that you have discovered your boss is selling the company?"

"All the options sound pretty interesting, but which is most beneficial to you?"

With this sort of response, your spouse will feel comfortable sharing more things with you because your words have shown that you are listening.

When your spouse feels comfortable talking about things with you, communication will be strengthened and it will lead to a happy home.

CHAPTER 8: Active participation to improve family communication

Family communication is simply the verbal and non-verbal exchange of information between all members of a family. This kind of communication involves being able to know what each family member is feeling, thinking or going through.

Family communication is a lot more complex than that of couples alone. This time it is a different ball game, particularly when children are involved in the family.

Being able to carry everyone along in your family and ensure effective communication can be very challenging. But If you are willing to pay the price that it requires, you will overcome all hindrances.

If communication is active within the family, it will lead to a greater family bond. The level of interaction among family members reflects in the satisfaction they have been members of that family.

Through communication, you can ascertain the different temperament of every family member and know how not to upset each other. How easily a conflict is resolved is determined by how great communication has been within the family.

When you meet someone who says "I have not spoken to my folks in months", you should know there is a faulty communication right there. Happy and healthy families keep in touch with each other.

Make your family a Priority if they are

It is not so difficult to make it obvious that your family is the center of your world. Simply place them above every other thing that least matters to you.

The way you celebrate their big wins, the empathy you show in their failures and disappointment, the surprises on their birthdays and their special days.

There is a clear difference between a child whose family attends his graduation and the other who only had a concerned neighbor come around. If his family refused to attend due to negligence, or because they feel it's not so important, the message of "you're not so important" has been passed.

The things you do and the things you don't do matters a lot in projecting your love for your family. When the family is a priority to you, make sure you to do your best at all times to please them, even if it is something as small as going to a dentist's appointment with your sister.

Be deliberate about making sacrifices for your family, let the words of your affections towards them correlate with your actions. Don't just say I love my family, action speaks louder than voice.

When you do certain things, people would already validate your true love for your family. You will hear comments like

"He has a good heart, he cares a lot about his family"

" You don't mess up with his sister, he'll come for you"

"She is such a loving mother, she can go any length for her children"

"He does multiple jobs just to make sure his kids are in school"

All of these statements sound like commentaries from a long term observation. When you genuinely love your family, all of your actions will point to the fact that they are a priority to you.

Opening Effective Communication Lines

You may be interested in changing your lifestyle to improve family communication but you are clueless as to what exactly to do and how to make your efforts visible to your family members.

Here is the thing, if you have not been very active in interactions within your family, it won't happen like magic. It will take some time before your efforts begin to show and correct the wrongs that have been done due to poor communication.

But hey! You can still make a difference

Eat Together

As simple as this sounds, it is a great effective communication tool. You can adopt the famous weekend dinner that is common among families. Some families make it a duty to eat dinner together on Sundays, it is not optional, it is made a family obligation, so family members are under compulsion to be there, particularly for adult children who no longer live with their parents.

What does this do?

People unwind the activities, challenges, and testimonies of the week during dinner.

For spiritual people, they pray together before dinner

Family members chat, laugh and share jokes

Major announcements like engagements, promotion, new employees are often shared during family dinner

And the beautiful thing about this routine is that communication is more open and clear such that family members look forward to days like this.

Beyond weekly dinners, it will also be interesting to share one meal as a family, particularly if the kids are still young. Children take advantage of the attention of their parents at the meal table to share gist about their academic successes and struggles, bullies and new student in the block.

The family that eats together, stay together.

Engage in periodic Private Talks

In as much as group discussions and dinners can be quite interesting and beautiful, some issues require private attention. A member of the family may not feel comfortable talking about something to the entire family just yet due to fear, anxiety or disappointment in themselves.

So to get into the situation in everybody's life, you can engage them in personal dates, you can take a walk down the street or even go to a public park and ask open-ended questions over ice cream and pizza.

Don't ask leading questions; be liberal in your questions, so they don't feel like they are being interrogated by some detective.

Take young children to fun sports and while they are devouring their favorite chocolate, ask them questions and in that excitement, they will tell you all that you need to know right there.

It may be difficult to share struggles with bedwetting over a family dinner you know! But by all means, ensure communication is getting stronger, and family bonds stronger.

Be an Active Listener

When a family member is trying to share information, either personal or general, try to listen to them. Being an active listener cannot be over-emphasized.

When listening, make sure you are not distracted by some other things within that space. This includes putting off the Television set, putting your phone away or facing the screen down so as not to be distracted by notifications of messages on your social media pages.

If you were previously listening to music on your headset, it will be nice to remove it. That way, your child, spouse or sibling will be confident with the fact that you are listening to what they have to say.

Another way to show that you are listening is by paraphrasing what you've been as a response to the discussion before airing your opinion. That way, the person will feel you are involved in their conversation and will feel safe coming back to share any issue because of their assurance in you that you always listen.

This also has a way of helping children in this kind of family listen, because they have noticed that whenever they talk, they are being listened to, so they will naturally learn to be attentive when being spoken to too.

Be Objective when dealing with Issues

Don't attack the personality, attack the problem at hand. When there are issues in the family, if you are not sure of maintaining calmness while talking about it, give it some time and allow your anger to wear out before you discuss it.

Address the wrong action, don't nail it to the personality, be careful of "Labeling". When you keep labeling a child, over time those words begin to form a perception about that child and become his or her identity.

Instead of saying "why are you such a failure"

You can say "Why did you fail that exam?"

Show unconditional love when addressing a matter, such that the person you are talking to understand that you are only concerned about them becoming better. Be careful not to start enmity with a sibling over an issue.

Some people refuse to talk to family members for donkey years because a particular issue was not properly handled. Do not spill hate in the process of correcting someone, else your intention will be misunderstood.

Scheduled Family Vacation

Amidst life business, it will be too exhausting not to have a minimum of one family vacation in a year. It doesn't have to be to an expensive location, you can save up for it.

Do something fun with your family away from Home! This creates enough time for family bonding, you can go skating together, boat rides, swimming, see animals in the zoo or parks, see life from a different perspective with your family in it.

While on some trips, you can do some evaluation. Ask your children what they think you have done wrongly all year long, tell your parents how you wish to be treated better, have those soul to soul conversation about your family life.

You will be amazed at how refreshed and renewed your communication life would be by the time you are back from your trip.

Show Appreciation

Be kind with words and show appreciation. Irrespective of who shows kindness to you. Learn to say thank you often, it is simple courtesy.

Celebrate all wins, either big or small. If your little son scores highest in numeracy, talk about it to everyone in his presence, when he feels appreciated for that little, he will be motivated to come top of his entire subject and class.

Show genuine kindness and love to every one member of your family. The language of love is easily communicated through deeds.

Always Keep In Touch

Different techniques have been made available for you to keep in touch with your family members, there is no excuse.

Through your mobile phones, you can reach out to your son who is in another state schooling.

You can speak to your wife from the office and check how her day is going.

You can check in on your husband's itinerary to prepare a special dinner while at work

You can call up your child's school teacher and send them lovely messages to encourage them

Through video calls, you can see bring your loved one back home from their trip mile away.

Do not break the line of communication because a loved one is not at around you, use technology to your advantage and ensure communication is still active irrespective of location.

Another benefit of optimizing technology for communication is that you also teach children around you that distance is not a barrier to keeping in touch and showing love. They will also learn to call you when you are away from home, they already understand that through those means, they can still show affection without physically seeing you.

They become confident of the fact that even when they go far away to school, through technology, you will also keep communication alive, and that gives some sort of assurance and security.

 It can be better

You may be wondering what you can do if communication is already very poor in your family. This may be difficult to amend because there might be underlying issues that are responsible for the bridge in communication and distance. First, you may have to discuss and resolve every issue, without this, communication may never be open.

After you have successfully resolved every difference, you can start to employ means to improve communication.

What more can you do?

You can start by calling your family members daily or weekly

Organize family get-togethers

Plan a family vacation

Do a homecoming for your parent's anniversary or remembrance as the case may be

An effective family communication leads to a healthy and happy family life. The world is getting too busy to live an isolated life. Keep communication alive and active with your family to enjoy the peace and joy that comes with family love. The truth is that genuine happiness is not in the houses or cars that you buy, or the gadgets you have, it is in the sincere affection, love and cares that you enjoy from family and friends.

Communication is not a passive thing, it is active. To get it right in the home, you must engage actively in the exercise. There is no limit to the amount of exercise you can adopt. Nobody should be left out in the game, remember, this is a family thing and you must handle it as such.

CHAPTER 9: Spicing up your relationship: speak the love language

Experiencing love with the right person is one of the beautiful things life can offer. In as much as you want all the love and attention, you want all the care, you want to enjoy all the benefits of falling and being in love, it will be great to be interested in reciprocating how your partner makes you feel to him or her.

Certain things can be done to spice up your relationship

Act Like you just met

It's possible to get bored with each other when you do the same things every day without adding a little spark to your love life. Pretend like you just met and do the same things you did at the beginning that made your partner fall in love with you.

Go out on romantic dinner where you fill the atmosphere with love

Talk a long walk and act like it's just the two of you in the world

Kiss yourself more often

Send flowers and chocolate to your partner's workplace

Having lunch together isn't a bad idea too

Talk about each other's interests and goals.

Some of the things sparked the fire from the onset, if you can do them again, your already boring relationship can be active again.

Have sex more Often

Poor Sex life can be boring. Some people have reduced sex to only weekends, or once in a week. Sex should be scheduled, because you may end up having it according to schedule, not because you are actually in the mood.

Be spontaneous, go with the flow, make out on your couch, in the car, at the bathroom, and at unplanned times. It helps you keep the fire rekindled.

Research on different "convenient" sexual positions that you have never tried out before, the emphasis is on convenience, because if it's not convenient for you and your partner, it may start killing his or her sexual drive. If your partner is not finding anal sex pleasurable, you may both have to look for other erotic styles to adopt.

Be sure that your sexual drive compliments each other, when one is tired or not in the mood, you can try a little foreplay and romance to ignite passion, never force sex on your partner.

Sending a sexy or flirty message during the day can be a romantic prep for great sex at the close of work.

Spend more time together

Make sure to spend enough time with your partners irrespective of how busy you get at work. Even if it's just to lay on each other's arms over a bottle of wine and see a movie.

Most times the things that matter in a relationship go beyond the expensive gifts that you think of, time is invaluable and so is the investment of it in a relationship.

Show your partner that beyond your job, they mean more to you.

Go on Vacation with your Partner

Vacations have a way of distracting you from work and all other pressure to the one you are with. When you experience beautiful places with someone you love, the memory lingers for long.

When you talk about the things you did together while on vacation, the beautiful memory has a way of flushing the romantic moments you had down to the present, and it boosts your love life.

To add spice to your relationship even while on vacation you can decide to wear your partner's favorite cologne, wear his or her favorite color, wear sexy lingerie and maintain a happy and romantic mood.

Go on separate Vacation

As much as a vacation as a couple can be a lot of fun, it's nice to go on separate vacations with a couple of friends. If your partner is going to Paris with his friends, you can decide to go to Dubai with your friends.

The time spent apart has a way of making your heart grow fonder of each other and it also helps you concentrate on the uniqueness of your partner which you may have forgotten, or gotten too used to.

The distance helps you appreciate the gift of love, friendship, and togetherness that you have probably taken for granted.

By the time you are back from your trip, you will see your spouse in a different light, he or she will appear like you are just meeting them for the first time. Everything will feel brand new and that's beautiful to spice your relationship and rekindle the fire of love between both of you.

Public Display of Affection

If your spouse is not embarrassed by PDA, feel free to hug them in the mall, steal a kiss, yeah!

Bringing your relationship to the open with a display of affection comes with a lot of assurance and intentional love, particularly when your partner has some insecurities about your relationship.

Understanding the 5 Love Languages

Physical attraction is personal, the same way love language is natural. What appeals to one person is different to some other people. That is why you don't love two different people the same way. There is always something peculiar and unique about every individual, so you should study your partner to know what love language works for him or her.

Don't assume the same things that appealed to your ex will also appeal to them. If you want to ask, you can ask, but if you want to know you can try out the whole five love languages and see which suits them the most.

In case you are not sure of what love language is, here are the 5 major love languages that have been transforming relationships in positive ways

1. Words of Affirmation

Words of affirmation are simply is saying words of appreciation and admiration to your partner to affirm your love for him or her. If your spouse is easily swayed by words that might just be it. Words that build your partner and fetch you more affection. These words don't have to be an epistle, it can come so short and simple.

Sweet words like

"You look stunning"

love your hair"
- are the most amazing woman in the world"

- make love so easy for me"

As happy as these lovely and pleasant words can make them is the same way a negative comment can ruin their happiness.

People whose love language is the word of affirmation generally give big meanings to every word you say.

What people say, not just you get to them and so you must be very careful with the kind of things you say around them.

You should be careful not to pass a comment to your spouse if his or her love language is words of affirmation. They can keep reminiscing on exactly how you said those things and be hurting for days, weeks and months until further positive and romantic words are deposited enough to take away the hurt.

Words generally get to them so easily, so if I were you, I will speak beautiful words always to spice up that beautiful relationship.

2. Receiving of Gifts

Who doesn't want to wake up to a box of chocolate and perfumes by the bed stand?

Some people fall deeper in love when their partners send them gifts.

If your partner's love language is this, it simply means your spouse feels more loved and appreciated when you give him or her gifts.

It doesn't have to be something you break the bank for, it can be as simple as a Nutella spread that she loves just to brighten her day or a simple notepad to keep records of his daily activities.

When you are deliberate about giving them a particular gift that they love or have been craving, it comes highly appreciated. What you have shown is that your partner is in your thoughts.

Most of the time people misinterpret this to mean their spouses' being materialistic, this far from it. The minute you assume this, you'll miss the point. And this may cost you your relationship.

3. Spending Quality Time

This type of love language involves wanting to spend quality time with your spouse, no televisions, no games, no friends around, just the two of you. The amount of time you spend with him or her validates the love you share.

Not much is expected from you, just your company at all times. As simple as this sounds, it can be a lot. Particularly if you have a job that is time demanding, you will have to help your partner understand the demands of your job while you spend every spare time with him or her.

If you are a medical doctor, for example, you may have to help your partner understand the nature of your job in cases of emergency outside your regular work time. But be sure to make the best of every time you share.

When you cancel on a date on your partner whose long language is quality time, make sure to give an adequate explanation as this can get your partner frustrated. You don't want to be seen as prioritizing the reason for your excuse over your partner as this can lead to a major misunderstanding.

- Go on romantic dates for just the two of you!

- see a movie!

- skating!

- swimming!

Do fun things and put your partner at the center of your world such that when you are not available, the beauty of the things you have done together will suffice for your absence. In summary, make every moment count.

4. Physical Touch

People with this type of love language, place a priority on kisses, hugs, holding of hands, hands around their shoulders, not necessarily sex.

If their partner is far away, they are easily frustrated. This is the "out of sight is out of mind" syndrome."

Nothing in the world can you give to satisfy their emotional cravings. They just feel more loved when you are around them and you touch them physically.

To people like this, going on a separate vacation will be a total waste of time and resources as their enjoyment is in the arms of their loved ones.

Having sex is not the ultimate goal, if you have a partner who loves to feel you physically, you will be surprised that they will even get clingier after sex.

What this kind of partner simply wants is for you to just always be there.

5. Act of Service

This kind of love language is doing physical things that your partner will love.

Like breakfast in bed, cooking, doing their laundry, picking a cheque on their behalf, cleaning the house and so on.

It requires a deep thought as to what exactly you can do to make your partner happy and doing it to make them feel more loved.

It should be done with your spouse's utmost interest in the long run. Because when your partner is happy, you are also at peace.

There are 5 different love languages, and all of them in their unique ways make you understand love more uniquely as relating to your spouse. When you and your partner understand what love language works for both of you, it will foster a stronger bond between both of you.

Constant communication

When you meet someone for the first time, or you're new in a relationship, the only way you can get very familiar with them is if you constantly talk about the things that you both love, the things that you detest, the things that make you grow fonder in love.

It's also good to talk about your mistakes of the past relationships; it guides your partner not to play on the things that you are sensitive to.

Constant and continuous conversations will help you settle into your new relationship without offending each other too often.

You make your partner your best friend when communication is effective, even if your love tank drains out through one or two misunderstandings, the active communication that has been established between the two of you will help you refill and love again. Most of the time, couples fall out because they cannot effectively communicate their likes and dislikes with each other.

There is a language of love. It can be verbal, nonverbal or symbolic. As examined above, the five languages of love are beautifully designed to ensure a special type of communication is enshrined in the home to bond better, the healthier your communication, the better your relationship in the marriage.

PART III

BEST PRACTICE, CHANGE YOUR MIND!

Perfection doesn't come without practice. This is the best part in this book where you can learn the specific activities to improve your communication in the relationship. You may need to work on your mind to learn or unlearn those you have inculcated to learn what works for your communication to be effective.

CHAPTER 10

How to improve communication skills

The ability to communicate effectively is perhaps the most valuable asset you can have in life. Your private, as well as public life, depends on it. You may be the best qualified for the job but your poor communication can mess things up for you in the interview.

You may have a good heart but your courtship can turn out to be a nightmare with a single statement your utter shattering everything.

Words are powerful and communication is the channel by which they reach others.

How well you can pass across your message goes a long way to how people will want to come around you.

Having good communication skills stand you out in the crowd to make the difference anywhere you find yourself. The abundance of communication skills you have in your arsenal has a lot to say about your abilities to build good relationships.

Communication skills: What they are

Consider communication skills is a collection of activities that helps you with your public performance in terms of expressing and passing your thoughts across to others.

Effective communication helps to understand people, situations and conditions around us. Communication helps to build trust with people, it is the tool you need to solve problems and share ideas with others.

In the business world...

Employers see great value in communication as they believe internal communication is one of the ingredients to boost productivity.

What communication skills have you built up in life to enhance your relationship with people?

Any of the following skills:

- Verbal communication skills
- Visual communication skills
- Good interpersonal communication skills
- Presentation skills
- Writing skills
- Listening skills

And a whole lot of other communication skills that will help you build solid relationships with loved ones, the community where you live, and your workplace and among family members and friends.

Though we grow up naturally with these communication skills, it takes conscious effort to develop them. That is why you find some people in the society who communicate their thoughts clearly while others may not be as good. It takes some work if you're not a good listener to start listening instead of wanting to talk all the time.

How well are you able to listen because the whole of effective communication starts right from here? It is a must-have skill.

By possessing strong communication skills, one can better connect with colleagues, friends, loved ones, spouse and the workplace staff.

Why improve good communication skills?

Though simple in its terms, communication, when not understood, can lead to conflict and destroy a relationship. You need to improve your communication ability because it deepens your relationship with others. Good communication helps you with good decision making. Communication can make you better.

So, how do you improve communication skills?

Experts in the communication field have explored proven ways on how to improve communication skills. Linda Reynier, Simon Lancaster and a host of others all have something to say about how effectively you can improve your communication skills.

Speak up

Be the initiator of the communication. It begins with someone. Take the bold step and the responsibility to start it. Don't hide behind the digital landscape, come out of your shell and speak up your mind clearly and concisely.

Be ready for the conversation

You won your thoughts and should be able to process them better. Think before going ahead to speak. If you're going for a speech, spend some time to prepare things, work on the draft. You can do a mockup conversation before you go for an event you'll be presenting.

Be ready for questions and answers

As already discussed, questions and answers, are key to communication. When you ask questions, it shows that you truly understand what the other person is saying. Don't assume you know what your partner is saying. Get clarification and find out exactly what should be known.

Have a grip of nonverbal communication

Nonverbal communication is a strong force when dealing with communication. When you have this skill around to work with, you can be sure to be up there with your communication. It accounts for 55% of how a group of listeners perceives their presenter. Even if you are that strong with your words, most of what you say does come from these words but via your physical cues.

To effectively communicate, the gestures, facial contacts, and the likes are boosts to how your communication can be effective. Avoid arm folding, don't appear smaller than who you are. Make sure to fill up space around you. Don't be static, move within the space around you. let your audience read meaning to what movements you make with parts of your body.

Cut down on visual aids

Visual aids are good, don't get it wrong here. But overdependence on them has overtime hampered real communication rather than help it. This is the reason Steve Jobs placed a rule banning PowerPoint presentation in its corporation. This was also followed by Sheryl Sandbergs decision to tour the same path with Jobs's stance at Facebook.

The point is that presentation tools like PowerPoint cut off the storytelling skills, use of compelling words and application of nonverbal cues for communication.

Be present in the relationship

To understand your partner during communication, you must be present. Be completely immersed in the communication realm by putting things aside that distract you. let him feel he has your presence, that you hold his presence as a number one priority in your life.

You can't improve communication in your relation things take your attention. They take away your awareness, being fully present, and mindful. Don't be too busy to not create the time to communicate effectively with your partner. Keep in mind that trust, love and good relationship virtues are builds during hard times and not when things are rosy with you in the relationship.

Honesty and open-minded is good

Good and lasting relationships don't thrive on falsehood. Say only what you mean, that comes from your heart and not from the mouth. Make your feelings clear, don't hide any. You can improve communication in your relationship by being open and honest. Doubts in a relationship kill good communication. Let your partner knows exactly who you are, be honest. Don't hide your weakness. Walking away from an argument is good ad a temporary way to deal with a communication problem. When you disagree, the virtues of honesty and trust won't make it hard for you to resolve issues in no time.

Timing is important

Most often people bring things up at the time they're angry or are feeling frustrated. It is not all the time you should bring up an issue. Only do this when you have sufficient time to discuss it. When you don't have the time to discuss fully, let it rest until when you have that time, else you'll be breeding confusion. Never approach your partner at a time when a more important issue is yet being resolved. Learn good timing for your communication.

There are many other aspects to improving communication skills. Specifically, the family unit should stand as a starting point to help improve this vital area of our everyday life.

CHAPTER 11

How to actively improve family communication skills

Communication is about everything in the family. It is the tool that has kept you together for this long. Every morning, you wake up to find everybody in the home getting about their businesses. While mummy is busy tidying up things around the home and preparing the kids for school, it is most likely to find daddy also getting set to hit the road for the day's work.

You'll most times hear your spouse's voice blaring to hurry the kids up not to be late, the verbal communication skill is more in use at this time of the day. Better communication skills in the family breed understanding and that's why you don't want to lose it when it comes to improving and communicating effectively in the family.

Poor skills in communication destroy emotional bonds and bring conflict among family members.

Good you're reading this book because there are tons of ways you can use to improve communication skills in the family and this is how.

Have time together with the family

Shift work periods, the overtime and business trips and among others can be standing on the way between you and your family spending quality time together. It is that easy not to have this time together if, for instance, both of you work long hours to meet the needs of the family. This doesn't leave out the kids as well. They are always busy too with school activities.

You can actively improve communication by having a forum where all members of the family meetup. Schedule a time.

Make it a priority to the point that everybody in the home will hold the time together as equally important as going for the day's work or attendance in school.

If you need to, adjust some activities you have scheduled for yourself to make way for the family's. These experiences won't come overnight; you have to consciously work at it. It may not come easily, expect some resistance, your grown kids may not find the idea convenient.

You just have to do it by setting the time aside for the family. How do you make it work? it should not be idle time. Your children and spouse should find the activities in it engaging. Make it conversational, let everybody be part of it, and make it fun. Play together, learn new things. Teach a topic on how to do a thing. They should want to participate in it. They should look up to it.

Eat Together

A good way you can improve communication in your family is to make sure you some of your meals together. it feels good when you have time together on the round table with every member of the family. Make it a regular schedule to have this experience. It can be a weekend thing or on special days like Sundays. I ask anyone around about how this has helped their family; you'll be amazed at the amount of feedback you'll get. Eating together encourages open communication among family members.

Have a family routine

Improving family communication comes by creating avenues that bring the family members together in one place. Family routines are engaging in activities. It can be a reading time where the children get to read a chapter in a book. Set aside a time for the movies at the cinema, go outdoors together, visit the museum and create fun activities that the children will love.

Getting these routines to work in the family helps the lives of everyone, creating stability in the home especially with the children. They'll look up to this day because it helps them to relax and creates a sense of anticipation among everyone. Routines this gives an opportunity for people to interact freely with others. Don't force things; try out many things to see what works and what doesn't before you stick to one.

Keep the connection via technology

This is the jet age and technology is driving many things. Leverage the power of these technologies to enhance the bond and communication in the family. Use social connections to keep in touch with your spouse and grown children. Have a family page on your favorite social media and frequently interact with one another.

This is more beautiful when you have children in college already. On the rare side, some families go to the extent of creating a website where everybody in the home has access to contribute their inputs. Your son can be that photography person who will want to post his collections. Your daughter may be a fan of poems who loves to post her lovely lyrics; this gives everybody a platform to do so. It is a place you can drive some positives and creativity into the lives of your children, let it work.

Strengthen Good Family Relationship

Improving communication comes with a good relationship. Keeping your relationship intact helps strengthen the bond between children and parents in the family. It as well lets parents get closer to each other along with the children. You don't need to preaching about good communication in the family when you have a family with good relationships.

Appreciate one another

Everybody loves kind words. Don't ignore the children when they perform excellently in the school. Reward their efforts. Celebrate them. Never forget their birthdays, make the special fr them. Your marriage anniversary is yet another, let your spouse feels she is special in your life. Be there for your children especially at periods when they are facing some challenges that have to do with their age. It is not wrong to criticize but do it with the motive to help members in the family improve. Is your son a football player, go visit him play in one of the games. Visit your daughter in one of her performances in the school choir. Appreciation and reward are essential parts.

Create a one-on-one time

True those family routines are great for many reasons, it is equally ideal to have one-on-one time together with each member of the family. It is not every discussion that is suitable for family time together. Your daughter will love a separate time with you as a mother to open up somethings about her or share the struggles she's passing through, give her the time.

Create a setting for this, let the atmosphere be a relaxing one. Use a neighborhood park to make them feel more at home and comfortable. Build trust in them in your discussion.

You should be there for your children. They should be free to call on your when they need to talk to someone, don't give them out to strangers. Make this part of your relationship a solid one that your children can fall on anytime they need assistance. Similarly, your friends make up a good part of your life. You will do well to also find ways to improve communication among them.

CHAPTER 12

How to communicate with friends better

Your friends are people who make your life interesting and fun. They have a significant part in your life. The strong connection you create through effective communication is key to helping you reach your desired goal in life.

You are responsible for your satisfaction in a healthy relationship. Any good friendship necessitates mutual trust and respect. Good communication is required to build and sustain a strong base for friendship. To interact well, you need to learn how well to listen, build confidence and manage any problems that might cause tension.

So, how do you communicate with friends better?

Listen

Listing comes up in every communication aspect and communication improvement with friends is no exception.

Most of us are talking more than listening, which makes us more preoccupied with what we're going to say more than what the other persons are saying. Take your time to listen to your friend's words, body language, and tone. Once they know that you listen to their thoughts and feelings, they would be more accessible and believe you. Ask any questions on what they mean to enable them to open their minds to you.

Be yourself, be real

Don't be another person or have two versions of you at different times.

Communication is achieved by being open and honest. The power to work through your emotions will help you connect with others. Say it the way it is. If you don't want to address a subject, say "I don't want to talk about it" to let the other party know where you stand. It can be a big step for others to know where you truly stand and they'll respect you for it. Small children are better at this because they haven't mastered all the psychological complexities of suppressing their emotions and being disappointed in their speech.

Match your words with actions

Telling your friend that she can still count on you is nothing unless you prove that this is the case with your actions. Once your friends know what to expect from you, trust becomes easier to establish and to maintain. For instance, you build trust by informing your friend, "I'll go to the gym with you," and afterward make that count by turning up with her weekly to lift weights. Your friend should know that she can believe your words because with your actions they have conveyed that to her.

Talk regularly

The secret to any healthy relationship is regular contact. No matter how busy your life may seem, do some time to chat frequently with your friends. Even if you only have a few minutes between activities or while driving in the car, pick up your phone and say hello. "Don't give more time to slip through without connecting," suggests Marie Hartwell-Walker. Talking to a friend regularly helps to keep the relationship intact.

With time, people grow and change and relationships undergo ups and downs. The more effort you bring into your relationship, the stronger it will become, and the greater the chance it will have to endure. Maintaining a relationship means making constant efforts. Strategies such as daily talks and healthy interactions will help build a solid, high-quality relationship that will stand the time test.

Spend time together

Not every friend has the opportunity to meet in person, particularly when the distance is a factor. But when possible try to see your mates face to face, even if it is inconvenient at times. That will reflect your dedication. It's important to talk on the phone or over the Internet, but it can't compare to being in your friend's physical presence. If your friend lives nearby, get together weekly or monthly. This will mean that you are constantly staring at each other to catch up. "All parties must dedicate themselves to maintaining and holding each other responsible for the relationship," suggests Ron Culberson

It needs maintenance to build strong, lasting friendships. With time, people grow and change and relationships undergo ups and downs. The more effort you bring into your relationship, the stronger it will become, and the higher the possibility it will have to endure. Maintaining a relationship means making constant attempts. Strategies such as daily talks and healthy interactions will help build a solid, high-quality relationship that will stand the time test.

Be honest

Lasting partnerships are built on trust, and trust comes from integrity. It's important that you be transparent to share your true feelings. If you're unhappy with your friend, talk about it. If you're humiliated by something that you've done, share it. If you are grateful for him helping out, let him know. Let him think that you respect him.

Actively listen

Like the USA State Department says, active listening requires finding interpretation rather than comprehension. Staying open and non-judgmental, focus exclusively on your friend and send nonverbal signals that you are doing what she says. Leave a moment for each assertion to sink in before answering. Ask questions for follow-up, and seek clarification where appropriate.

A good conversation is an art. Like any skill, this involves the constant practice of those who want to stay at the top of their game.

Use humor

Laughter creates good emotions and strengthens relationships, so, have it all over the interactions. Sweet, funny comments and in-jokes make you feel better about your relationship. Yet beware of not overdoing it. Your girlfriend wants a man who is respectful, professional and not a comedian for 24 hours. Unless you're sure she's comfortable with it, avoid making her the brunt of jokes, and tone down the humor when she's in a serious mood.

Have a balance in the conversation

When chatting with your friend, establish harmony in the conversation. Share what's going on in your life without concentrating the whole conversation on you. Please ask questions. Look for insights, and feedback from your friend.

Find out what's different in her life, or what she may need your advice. Show interest by talking about he interests or jobs. If your friend has one accomplishment, be appreciative. Hartwell-Walker states why, in contrast, good friends honor each other's successes without feeling jealous or weakened.

It requires care to build strong, lasting friendships. With the passing of time, people grow and change and relationships undergo ups and downs. The more effort you bring into your relationship, the stronger it will become, and the higher the possibility it will have to endure. Maintaining a relationship means making constant efforts. Strategies such as daily talks and healthy interactions will help build a solid, high-quality relationship that will stand the time test with a friend.

CHAPTER 13

20 communication exercises and activities

The resources in this piece include exercises, games and other activities that give you the opportunity to learn more about effective communication, help direct your relationship with others and develop your communication skills.

Some might sound like a chore that you need to mark off your to-do list while others might make you forget that you're not just having fun with your kids, but really improving vital life skills; but, they all have one thing in common: they'll help you become a stronger, more efficient and more optimistic communicator with those who matter the most to you.

While making your interactions smoother, good communication exercises also have relationship-building benefits: effective communication demonstrates the other person's respect and value.

The Value of Communication Exercises

People have been trying to grasp the place of a healthy relationship for decades.

Over the years, numerous hypotheses have been proposed by researchers and experts to determine whether a partnership would make it down the street, or whether it has the potential to persevere through old age.

Despite differences of opinion, contact is generally agreed that the secret to demystifying and unlocking the padlock is crucial.

Communication activities aim to improve each partner's verbal, non-verbal, and written communication abilities, in addition to promoting interpersonal communication growth.

Practitioners encourage partners to participate in contact drills at least 2-3 days a week, allowing for stability and continuity.

If a couple is taking part in therapy, the therapist will often give conversation tasks as "homework" assignments to allow partners to learn new techniques in between meetings.

The best practice advises partners to work on and master one interaction area before heading to the next.

When it comes to improving communication, the old adage, "practice makes perfect" is very true.

Couples will feel secure by the dedicated commitment and regular practice when learning their new skills in a safe manner.

It allows us to understand each other better. This makes us feel more relaxed with each other and also facilitates better and more productive interactions. Specifically:

- Set aside the time to talk to others.
- Only talk about what you'd like to learn.
- Be clear about what you want to say.
- Keep your message clear so your companion correctly listens to it and knows what you say.

- Speak about what's going on and how that's influencing your life. Speak about what you want, need, and feel.
- Accept responsibility for what you say or do. Hear out your friend. For the time being, put aside your own emotions, and try to understand their motives, fears, needs, and desires -this is empathy at play. Share positive impressions with your friend.

Good marital contact can mean the difference between a long-lasting, happy relationship with minimal stress and one that is chaotic and end-destined.

Luckily for you, learning the techniques of conversation is something that anyone can do with enough practice.

And the best part of these exercises is that you can do them all from the comfort of your own home!

Read on to discover the best strategies and practices for partners in conversation that will help improve your communication skills within your relationship or marriage while also helping to build trust.

Communication Exercises

There are a number of contact activities to choose from, all addressing various vocal, nonverbal, and written competencies.

Verbal exercises encourage couples to express themselves using language which is polite.

Nonverbal activities help people learn the meaning and the resulting effect of body language, facial expressions, emotions, and eye contact.

Activities of written communication teach couples about speech through writing.

Notwithstanding the exercises try to restore communication and trust within the relationship. Types of communication techniques that involve visual, nonverbal, or written contact are included.

1. High-low Exercise

This verbal method in communicating allows individuals to express themselves freely, while their partner uses attentive listening strategies. It is like answering the question, "how was your day?"
Such practice should be used during the latter part of the evening. It helps couples to check the most important aspects of their day.
The partner is asked to share the best part of their day, their "high" part, and the most frustrating part of their day, their "low." As one partner expresses, the other uses active listening strategies to express empathy and understanding.

2. Listening without comments

This is an approach related to verbal and nonverbal contact. A timer is set for 3-5 minutes, and the chance for one person to verbalize what they think and feel without interference is given.
The other person, however, can use only nonverbal methods to express concern, appreciation, and motivation. The pair reviews the experience when the timer goes off by sharing thoughts, emotions, and ideas.

Each partner then changes positions to get a chance to practice both skills.

3. Eye Contact

This is a nonverbal method in conversation, focusing solely on eye contact. In this exercise, two chairs are put in calm, relaxing environment, facing each other.

Both parties are required to maintain five-minute eye contact, without looking away. During this exercise both of you are encouraged to enjoy the experience.

Couples are to explore their experience, degrees of relaxation or pain and body reactions at the end of the exercise.

Every person has the ability to imagine what their partner thought about determining communication and whether nonverbal signals come through or not.

4. Sit and write

This is a communication practice that focuses on written communication.

A blank postcard with instructions for writing a message expressing a disappointment, a thought, or a wish is offered to both partners.

Afterward, each partner is asked to use another postcard to write a response to the letter from their partner.

Trust-building exercises

In a partnership, one of the most important building blocks is that of trust.

Trust conveys emotional and physical security, which grows from truthful, consistent and straightforward contact over time.

One of "Titanic"'s most famous scenes shows Jack reaching out his hand to Rose, saying "Do you believe me? Confidence exercises can be carried out in everyday life in far less drastic situations but the principle remains the same. If a friendship is built on a strong foundation of confidence, it can survive almost any challenge.

5. Copycat

This operation is target-oriented and its performance is directly linked to the level of communication and trust among partners.

A couple is asked to sit with the same selection of building blocks backing each other.

One partner constructs a structure and is then given the opportunity to offer verbal instructions to the other partner to construct the same structure by trusting the other partner's guide.

That person needs to trust that their partner can give them straightforward, succinct and precise guidance so that they can achieve their goal successfully.

6. A helping hand

In this exercise, partners must work together to achieve a shared goal with an arm bound behind each back.

All parties need to concisely express instructions and acts so that each person can use their own free hand to reach the goal.

Any target, such as buttoning a coat, zipping a belt, securing a shoe, or fastening a necklace, may be used.

Exercises for engaged couples

Despite today's exorbitant rates of divorce, premarital counseling is becoming a more frequent and requested facility.

Couples are trying to improve their relationships before marriage through advice and experience in an attempt to avoid being a negative impact.

Communication exercises can be used with a mental health professional as part of premarital counseling or may be performed by the pair themselves.

These activities try to make people conscious of their own communication styles, while at the same time educating them about safer and more effective habits.

In fact, these practices aim to increase the bond and trust within their relationships.

7. Future goals and plans

Such practice helps a couple define and express future goals and desires within themselves.

In an effort to understand what each partner needs to be happy and satisfied within the relationship, partners are urged to consider and address short- and long-term goals.

8. Music

This practice requires the use of music and song to communicate itself.

Partner chooses three songs they will connect to, and then share their lyrics with their partner.

This exercise is intended to stimulate dialogue about why songs are important, the kinds of emotions evoked, and the motives for choosing a particular song.

9. In His/her Name

This type of exercise is meant to promote emotional communication, closeness, positive feelings, and appreciation.

For each letter of the partner's name, each person is asked to choose a complement or good attribute to characterize their partner.

The person is then asked to read their list, whilst explaining their effect on self-esteem, trust, and self-worth.

10. top 3s

The goal of this game is to consider the positive aspects of your relationship and the everyday activities that your partner does.

Set aside a few minutes to think about your day at the end of each day. Consider your partner's three best things for you on that day.

Next, take turns to remind you that they loved you so much.

The game focuses on appreciation and gratitude, two important and very often missed contact and interaction pieces. And don't forget to say, "thank you."

11. Closeness

This game is actually a take-off from the staring contests for most adult.

The aim of this activity is to make your partner more comfortable with expressing yourself. Being next to each other increases feelings of familiarity and connection. This game can be sexy.

So here's the game: Sit in front of each other so you're close enough to hold your hands.

Look straight into each other's eyes.

Note the emotions you feel.

Now start to talk about it. It may be about your day or something funny that happened at some other time.

Just let your spouse share something when you're done. Do this back and forth a few times.

12. Twenty questions

This is a fun and lightweight connecting game. Remember 20 Questions in the Game? This is an adult version.

Often we fail to heed the little things that make us who we are. Paying attention to and remembering the little details creates a sense of common awareness. Here's the game: Without distractions, set aside some time for you two.

Each of you should make a list of 20 personal questions before you sit-down, to ask the other. Be imaginative with the questions—dumb, serious, specific life or subject areas.

13. Dating exercise

Make a date with your partner to do something fun—something special, and maybe even somewhat spontaneous. The only ground rules are this: It has to be something for just the two of you and you can't talk about kids, work or home issues like that leaky kitchen faucet.

Choose something that demands that you're present. Go sailing, climb the rock, sneak away for a quiet weekend... there are endless possibilities.

Take turns to pick up the action. Surprise your friend with what's new.

The aim of this game is to reconnect in an activity that requires you both to be there for each other. You are going to be on neutral ground, away from home and job pressures.

14. Repeat and reverse

The game is more enjoyable when measuring patience and tolerance for the best of each other. Just sit back and relax in for this session. Now each has a turn to chat, the other should listen carefully while the partner is talking.
You'll need to choose subjects that cause trouble for you. It may be job, or housework, or even grocery, cats, lawn, and garden. Then the other has to address him/her after the companion, speaks and explains the topic in his / her own terms. This can be accomplished as a conversation when adding your own viewpoint as a reference to the repeated phrase.

15. Romantic glare

Now that may be the most loved out there for us. This is more of a love activity, with the couples being able to effectively improve communication. The pair will sit opposite each other, hold their hands and look in each other's eyes. Keep a minute or two to the time. Chat with your friend about the silliest things, or the most relaxed stuff. Start one by one, share opinions and questions like the best part of being with each other, the last movie or game you've played together. It can be as easy as how the day in office was, etc, but keep this quick.

16. Structured communication

Number one of the top 5 activities for partners in contact is formal dialogue. Set aside time to speak to your friend for this task, and pick a subject to explore.

Once a subject is chosen all partners will start talking. Instead of talking as you would usually, by using mirroring, affirmation, and understanding, build more meaning in the conversation. A simple, "I see what you're thinking" is okay. Eventually, sensitivity expresses interest in how the mate feels by saying something along the lines of, "How do you feel like that?" This is one of the best practices to improve communication skills and to instill a deep sense of empathy among couples.

17. Positive language

A positive language game is second on the list of relationship development and engagement games for partners.

Communication between spouses entails a lot of challenges. The biggest barrier to enhancing trust in a relationship is defensive, presumptuous, and accusatory behaviors.

This is one of the important tests in communication skills in which couples must substitute negative language with positive language.

The next time you're about to say something negative about their acts or attitudes of your friend, stop and come up with a more positive way to get your point across. It makes people more aware of how they communicate, which reverses negative forms of communication.

18. Sharing emotions

Another one of the couples ' bonding activities that partners will engage in is expressing their feelings among themselves.

This may not come easily for many and may take years for the two to share their feelings freely. To support and nurture your family, go on retreat for couples and share your innermost feelings and sitting side to side with each other. It will support your wife's understanding and make the union better.

Understanding and adhering to these techniques in communication will help partners cope with sensitive issues. Poor communication often does far more than hinder the ability to deal with daily issues.

A lot of communication issues occur because of a lack of mutual understanding. Play this game to know your partner better. You'll need tools that can help you build or develop. For example, clay, blocks, and boxes for kids, or even some crayons and map for that. Then sit down with your friend, face up to your backs and hug each other. Now, you just sit back-to-back. Everybody should take turns to describe in detail an image, structure, etc. The other should try using the definition to imagine and construct the closest possible object or illustration.

19. Using I Statements

Some of the problems sometimes found in interpersonal conversation is when words such as ' you could' are used in expressions. By using "I statements" you need to own your feelings. This may be very tough habit to establish but communicating effectively without creating a blame game and initiating a conflict is very important. You should exercise using I statements as part of your expression to show your commitment and responsibility rather than pointing accusations to the other party.

20. Sticks and stones

There is every reason to believe that it hurts to call one name. Relationships have their downs and lows and the issue of name calling can surface. Sticks and stones is an exercise that makes you discuss this. Call your partner to sit and ask that both of you list out the names you've called yourselves in the past. Discuss how you feel about them when used. The two of you now decide on ways to avoiding such in the future.

CONCLUSION

All lies in your hands right now to take the needed move to make the change that will drive change in your social, professional and personal life. Communication that is effective is the key to unlock a beautiful relationship that is built on trust, honesty, sincerity and happiness.

It is never too late to give effective communication a try in your relationship if it is the missing link for your relationship. If you're in a romantic relationship, you can't leave the importance of communication to chance in the relationship. Get practical and let your partner discover something new is coming on the way of your relationship.

It is hoped that the insightful exercises of this book including detailed explanations provided are sufficient to make the difference you need in your relationship and drive it to a desired height.

I'd love your HONEST feedback!
Let me know what you thought of this book!

Thank you

Printed in Great Britain
by Amazon

35963245R00069